40 Frenchie Foodie Stories

Short stories about everyday eating in France

Paris Connolly

40 Frenchie Foodie Stories
ISBN: 978-2-492620-42-3
Text by Paris Connolly.
Front cover graphic by funnymonk696.
Illustrations by Paris Connolly.

Paris Connolly is Australian, based in France.
This book has British spelling.

369FAD7410574CCC458009758186ACEF05FBFFDBFEDD5DE82F0E2A482BEEF174

"Eating is so intimate. It's very sensual.
When you invite someone to sit at your table
and you want to cook for them,
you're inviting a person into your life. "

— **Maya Angelou**

Foreward

I'd like to thank my French friends and acquaintances in this book for sharing food and happy moments. (Names have been changed.)

I moved to France about a decade ago. Prior, I was in the UK for years, and before that, Australia. I grew up on an Australian diet, and although I adore living and eating in France, I still appreciate a cheap hot dog or a supermarket slice of cheesecake. I don't know if this is going to go away.

Some terms I use a lot in the book, which you probably know but just in case:

Saucisson: *Saucisson* is dried, cured meat in a sausage shape.

Le Tabac: a shop which sells cigarettes, lottery cards, and sometimes books and souvenirs.

Foie Gras: duck or goose liver.

Baguette: the long, cylinder-shaped French bread.

Savoie: This is a region in France in which I have spent a lot of time. (As I'm typing this, I'm in Savoie, looking out at snow.) It's on the eastern side of France, next to the Italian border. People or things from the Savoie region are called *Savoyard*.

Arrondissement: District/Section/Neighbourhood of Paris. Paris consists of 20 *arrondissements*.

Finally, my name is Marie Connolly, and I refer to

myself as Marie in the book. Marie Connolly as an author name was already taken when I started writing the 40 Frenchie Series. So... Paris Connolly, here I am, at your service.

Right. It's your last chance to duck out if you are vegetarian or sensitive to animal food references (no pun intended). Otherwise, happy reading!

Paris Connolly

CONTENTS

1. WELCOME PÂTÉ

Macot, the Alps, Savoie.

Knock, knock.

I look at the door. Who? I don't know that many people yet. I've only just moved to this village. It's set at the base of a mountain. It has only one primary school where kids of different ages are grouped together in classes. Then, there's one mini supermarket and one bakery.

I look to the 60-year-old man at my door. He is my new neighbour. His black hair is as thin as he is. He wears jeans with a red checked shirt. He looks like he might have been the one to cut down the wood in my new apartment. It is one hundred percent wood, even the bathroom. Of course, that is the charm of the place. It has "Country Home!" shouting out from the decor. My new neighbour has "Farmer / Hunter!" shouting out from his decor. In his weathered hands, he holds a gift.

'Hello, this is for you.' His rough hands extend, offering me a jar.

My face opens in a huge smile.

My neighbour says, 'It's pâté. I made it.'

I take the jar. My eyes sparkle. 'Thank you. What type of pâté?'

'Deer.'

My smile freezes. 'Deer?' I look at my neighbour. I scan his tanned skin, deep wrinkles, rough hands, checked shirt, loose jeans, and work boots. I look back up to his face, past his black, thin-hair combover, and to the resplendent mountains behind him in the background. The mountain forest is lush, bursting with life. It is home to foxes, boar, badgers, and deer, including for sure, the originator of what I was now holding in my hands. I swallow. 'Did you, uhm, hunt this deer?'

Hunter/Farmer smiles and nods.

My voice goes on *polite mode*. 'Wow! You hunted the deer. Then you made pâté from that deer.' I'm verbalising as I'm processing. 'Well, well.' I bow my head, 'Thank you.' I smile my most gracious smile.

The man bows and backs away. I close my door, walk back inside, and place the jar on my wooden breakfast bar which is covered in lists of French verbs. The word *Manger* sticks out from the lists. This is the verb: To Eat. I know that I will not *mange* this pâté, which is crazy because I love meat. I will eat kidneys, livers, and tongue, but unfortunately I have a clear picture of Disney Bambi, and I know I cannot eat this pâté. Shit.

The next day, I open my front door and almost step on a lettuce laying on my stone doorstep. It's not a whole lettuce. At least, not as I know it. I'm Australian and grew up in the suburbs where we shopped in fluorescent-lit supermarkets and bought fat lettuces. This lettuce on my doorstep looks like a distant poor cousin lettuce. It is long and thin. It looks like it's missing about 77 leaves. Next to it, sit four red tomatoes. They look like poor cousins too, ones that didn't know that tomatoes are supposed to grow in a round shape. These guys are wonky-shaped. They grew up and down, and left and right. Next to the four wonky-shaped tomatoes are two long spring onions. Normal-looking. But just two. I reach down, pick up my smorgasbord, and go back inside.

I know who put these vegetables on my doorstep. It's the lady who lives in the row of farm chalets behind my place. She has a plot of land separate to her chalet, which is her vegetable garden. She has come before, bearing equally minimalist-looking articles of food. I make no mistake though, because the food may look minimalist, but this produce would sell for much at the Bio markets. Bio markets are popular, and the prices are astronomical. So, I appreciate the lady with the white hair. Her husband I appreciate less, mind you, because I ran into him and another older neighbour when I got back from my bike ride the other day. I was climbing the steep path up to my front door when the two men stopped to joke around with me. The first one said to the other one, 'And your wife?' (referring to the lettuce lady). The second man, with neatly brushed hair and well-pressed clothes, made a fist. He placed his fist in the bent elbow of his other arm. My eyebrows had shot up because he had made an F-U sign, whilst laughing with his mate. He had put such energy into that sign that my senses had gotten quite the shock but I managed to keep the smile plastered on my face. Internally I'd rolled my eyes, however, and then I'd internally sighed. Boys will be boys, but then they will someday be men, and somehow still be boys. Oh, how they will make themselves laugh.

Anyway... back to my kitchen bench. Thank you lady for

your homegrown lettuce and goodies. I know how I'm going to eat this. Each time I eat at my French friend's house, she serves the main meat meal first, and then she serves the salad afterwards, separately. And the salad isn't salad as I know it: tomato, onion, corn, olives, feta cheese, you name it, all thrown in. Salad is just lettuce leaves, with vinaigrette. Not vinaigrette out of a bottle; it's oil, vinegar, and good quality mustard mixed together.

So, I look at the skinny, poor-cousin lettuce before me, and nod. I know what to do with it. Now to think of something for the wonky guys and the two good-looking spring onions.

The phone rings. It's my friend, Rose. I tell her about the deer pâté.

'Ooooooh!' she says.

I hear the delight in Rose's voice and suddenly, I know where the deer pâté is going. My sister said to me a long time ago, "Marie, you don't know how to share." Well, guess what? Today is the day.

2. LE SAINT-HONORÉ

Saint-Ouen, Ile De France.

The *Saint-Honoré* has been on my mind all morning. It's my new favourite dessert. It's a pastry consisting of a little tower of profiteroles sitting on a custard-lined base. Fresh cream nestles in and around the profiteroles. I drool. I should have gone straight to the *Saint-Honoré* first, but I thought, "Oh, the shops will be opening up again (after being closed because of Covid). It will be nice to stroll along the boulevards and window shop. I'll grab my *Saint-Honoré* on my way home."

I get off the metro at Saint Lazare station. I hate Saint Lazare Station. It's busy and chaotic. The design is all wrong. It's as if the designers specifically want crowds of rushing people to crash into each other. It's a human obstacle course.

For some reason, today I choose to change and take a second metro from Saint Lazare to Grand Boulevard Metro, instead of walking like I usually do. I follow the arrows in the tunnel towards Green Line No. 9. I turn the corner and see three Metro Inspectors. My stomach sinks. It's too late to turn back. They've seen me.

Let's backtrack a bit. The situation is: we've been in Covid confinement in Paris for like forever. There have been no inspectors on public transport in ages. I am unemployed. I'd figured, "I'll buy some reduced tariff tickets. I'm unemployed, and nobody is checking anyway." Let me say, I have never done this before. Let me also say, I know that in order to buy the reduced tariff tickets you need to provide a little card that says you are entitled to the reduced tariff. I also know very well that I don't have that card, and I don't feel like getting it because I don't even know how to apply for it. Plus, I am in Paris temporarily. I took the risk.

Today, that risk bites me on my big behind.

'That will be a fine of 35 euros, Madame. You can pay by card or cash.'

'I don't have 35 euros.'

'Then we'll take your details, and you will have two months to pay. But it will be 45 euros.'

In my head, I'm thinking that in two months I'll be able to provide proof that I'm unemployed and contest the fine.

'Okay.'

'Sure?'

'I don't have the option.'

She proceeds to take my address and details. Meanwhile, commuters are passing by. They show their tickets to the two other inspectors. I keep my head down, not wanting to make eye contact with anyone. I have become "one of those people," the kind good citizens shake their heads at. I've become one of those people where others think, "Cheater! Cheater! Look, she got caught. Good!"

The shame builds in my heart, and my head hangs low. I take the ticket from the woman. 'What happens now?'

'You will get the fine in the mail. You have two months to pay 85 euros.'

'85?!!' I look at the woman. 'I thought you said 45?' I look at the tiles on the tunnel wall, then back to the inspector. I'm going to have to swallow it. I say, 'And now it's too late?'

'No. You can go and get your cash. We'll be here for another 45 minutes.'

Rather than lose face and tell her that I actually have a fifty-euro note snuggled in my jacket pocket, plus my bank card in my purse, I tell her that I will be back with the money. Then, I turn and walk back through the tunnel, and fill in time by walking around and around like a dickhead inside the chaotic St Lazare station.

I'm tempted to go out of the Metro station but am too scared to go out because my all metro tickets are reduced tariff (I bought a packet of ten!), and what happens if I get caught again coming back in? My head is hot. My heart races. Oh, this is shit. Oh, I feel shame. Oh, I am kicking myself. At the same time, the optimist in me is trying not to overreact. The optimist is trying to see the funny side. But frankly, I could have spent that money getting sports shorts. I really need those shorts. Shit. Shit. Shit.

Fast forward to two hours later, and I'm standing in front of the bakery section in my local Saint-Ouen supermarket.

I look at the individual, one-person-size *Saint-Honorés* in the display window. They are lined up one behind the other. Each *Saint-Honoré* has three profiteroles. Each profiterole is lined with a thin base of hard toffee that cracks as you bite into it. The very top profiterole is decorated with a little chocolate oval and almond flakes.

The man in the bakery hands me a pretty little box with my dessert inside. 'Anything else?'

I look at the display. This could be one of those days where I eat two desserts. I know myself. I'm feeling down. I'm going to want a second one. Which one? They're all amazing: chocolate slices tiered with different types of chocolate, strawberry *tartelettes*, and lemon meringue *tartelettes*. I can't decide. I remind myself that I also have a block of dark chocolate in my shopping basket. I look at the server. 'That will be all.'

At the registers, I pay and pick up my shopping bag with the *Saint Honoré* box sitting on the top. My shopping is heavy. I decide to take the bus home. I hold two euros in my hand to pay the driver, but the driver shakes his head. Drivers are not taking money anymore. One must buy a ticket before getting on the bus. My heart sinks. My shopping bag is heavy. The driver sees the dilemma written over my face, and he kindly nods for me to get on the bus. I step on and take my seat. At each subsequent bus stop however, I fidget and sit up straight as I look to the doors, expecting transport inspectors to get on and fine me all over again. At each stop, I bite my bottom lip, and tap my feet. My knees bump up and down. The tension gets worse and worse as we travel along. The bus ride is a time bomb. I can't take it. I stand and ring the bell. I get off the bus halfway through the journey, and walk the last twelve minutes home, lugging my heavy shopping. I feel like I've earned this punishment. Bad transport cheater, bad transport cheater, bad transport cheater.

I get back to my apartment, sweaty and tired, but having made peace in my head and having forgiven myself for being a cheater because I know I will never do it again.

After my evening meal, I place my *Saint-Honoré* on a china plate. I take the top profiterole, study it, then bite into it. Fresh cream oozes into my mouth and mixes with the cracked toffee. My eyes flutter. I savour the bite. It is delicious. I take another bite, and another. I pick up the next profiterole and eat it. Finally, I look at the remaining profiterole sitting in the pastry base. I consider stopping eating, then having the rest tomorrow. That thought lasts for two seconds. I take another bite. My eyelids flutter even more as I savour the delicious French pastry which normally costs 3 euros, but today cost an extra thirty-five. *Mmmmmmm. Goooood.*

3. BILINGUAL SCHOOL

Lyon, Rhône-Alpes.

(it's a lettuce)

A teacher calls out. 'Children! Line up!'

These kids don't need to be told to line up. They do it automatically.

It's lunchtime and I'm standing in the school dining hall. The canteen staff buzz around like bees behind the food counter. They wear white net caps on their heads and blue gloves on their hands. They stock cool steel shelves with yoghurts and chocolate eclairs. Next to the cool shelves, they fill up the hot food section. Today, there is a fish or beef choice. Then, next to the hot bay marine, there is the bread basket and me, the bread lady. My job is to hand out bread. I've hit the big time, right? This lunchtime duty doesn't bother me. I enjoy watching these mini-humans in their school canteen environment because the French way of eating fascinates me. These little Frenchies eat breakfast, lunch, dinner, and a snack at 4 pm. Apart from that, they don't snack. Not even after dinner. I taught at a Lyon university once and I asked my first-year engineering students, 'Don't you ever eat after dinner? Like, *ever*?'

They raucously said, 'Yes! Sure! Sure we do.'

'Yeah? Like what?'

The 18-year-old in the front row with sandy-blonde hair flopping over his forehead held his thumb and forefinger together, and said, 'A little biscuit. One.'

I'd internally rolled my eyes as I recalled my many midnight treats, and none of them included one of anything.

So, I'm standing at the canteen of this Lyon Bilingual School which has some beautiful old buildings, set in impressive grounds. The first day when I drove in, my eyes had swept across the enormous green lawns, and up to the large main building set further back. The whole estate is grandiose, yet welcoming. The canteen is in a separate building, to the right. Large windows look out to the green football pitch. Inside, I stand by the bread basket, my blue-gloved hand outstretched, ready to hand out bread to these quintessentially French kids. I'm sure 4-year-old and 5-year-old kids are cute in all countries, but these little dudes are speaking in gorgeous French accents. How can one not crack? I'm going to, any minute now.

A little one comes up to me, holding his blue plastic tray with his yoghurt and fish dish.

I say in English, 'Bread?'

Little heads whip around when they hear my accent. I'm new to this school. The children don't know me yet. Their little eyes light up. My accent has pricked up young ears all the way down the queue. Kids reaching for their yoghurts on the cold steel shelves on the opposite side of the room are already looking over to me, then whispering to their friends. I see the curiosity on their faces.

The little boy in front of me says, in English, 'Yes, Bread, please. Thank you!'

More and more kids come to me with bright eyes and big smiles as they take their bread and say thank you. Some of them don't have the pronunciation yet, but they speak confidently, without hesitation or embarrassment. This is the beauty of getting kids to learn languages at a young age; they don't associate difficulty or obstacles to it. I'm loving it. They're loving it. They say, *'Merci!'* to the French lady behind the bay marine, then they turn to me, and, in English, say, 'Yes, one bread please.'

'There you go!' I place a piece of baguette on the plastic tray and watch the little one ever so carefully carry his big tray of food to the table.

The next child comes forward with her tray. She's four, and has a head full of golden curls. She wears a pleated navy skirt past the knees, grey socks, and black babydoll shoes. She smiles at me. I'm about to crack. She's just too cute. She says in a loud voice, 'You speak the English!'

'Yes! I do!'

She laughs.

'Would you like bread?' I say.

She nods. I put a piece of bread on her tray, and she smiles again, walking away with the tray that is almost as big as her. She says, 'Thanks.'

I raise my eyebrows. "Thanks," not even "Thank you." Very good.

Once the little kids are seated and eating, the 6 and 7-

year-olds come in. They are old enough to get their own bread, so I am called into the dining room next door to stand by the salad bar, again, to help the 4 and 5-year-olds.

The square salad bar has rice salad, potato salad, couscous salad, slices of ham, slices of salami, lettuce leaves, and vinaigrette.

A 5-year-old comes up, holding a little side plate. He gazes across at the different food in the salad bar. He gazes, and gazes, and gazes. Eventually, he says (in English), 'Rice salad, please.' He raises his plate to me.

I take the large plastic spoon and put a spoonful on his plate. I ask him if he would like another scoop. He shakes his head.

'Anything else?'

He shakes his head.

Another kid comes forward with his side plate. He stares at the salad bar. I wait. He stares and stares. Patience is not a strength of mine, but I am fascinated at how seriously these little kids are taking their food choice.

Eventually, the little boy says, 'Salad, please.'

I point to the loose lettuce leaves. 'This salad?'

He nods.

I pick up a leaf and put it on his plate. I go to pick up a second leaf, and he says, 'No, it's okay.'

I look down at the one loose leaf of lettuce on his plate. 'Vinaigrette?'

He nods.

I decorate the one leaf in dressing.

He walks away, happy.

I stare after him, amazed that a young child has come, and out of all the stuff on the table, asked for a leaf of lettuce. So far, none of these kids have asked for more than two things. If that had been me, I would have been like, "Ham please, yes two slices, and salami, two slices, yes and rice salad, and a little potato salad, and a bit of couscous. No, no lettuce. Thank you!"

Next, another little boy walks up with his empty side plate. He stares at the table for a long time. Finally, he says, 'Salad, please.'

I nearly drop to the floor. Seriously? These 4-year-old kids?! They've gotten a taste for lettuce leaves! I don't understand it. Their parents aren't here. They are not forced to eat lettuce, yet they are willingly choosing to eat green leaves. They like it. They like the vinaigrette that goes with it, too. *And*, they are eating their salad after they've finished their main course of fish or meat. There is an order to things in France which I'm slowly learning. I'm also slowly learning how eating food is a learnt skill just as learning another language is. They are learning to eat balanced meals and widen their palates in a most impressive fashion. I am in awe. Impressive buildings, impressive grounds, impressive food choices.

4. FIRST TIME SEEING DONKEY SAUCISSON

(not a euphemism)

Bourg Saint Maurice, the Alps, Savoie.

I have landed a job in Savoie for a ski company. The office sits in an alpine village called Bourg Saint Maurice. It's a three-hour drive from Geneva or Lyon airports. I am immediately charmed by the village. As I look around, I feel like exclaiming, 'Ooooh la la la la!' because I feel like I am walking in old-world France. The village is set in a valley, surrounded by tall mountains. The tops of those tall mountains nestle ski resorts, and each night, as darkness falls, lights twinkle into life.

The architecture of the houses and businesses in my new alpine village fascinate me because I come from Brisbane, where most buildings are made of glass and steel. Here, as I walk around, I note the old old old old old *old* stone houses and buildings. I also note the cobbled stones under my feet. Wow. This is proper old, and proper traditional. My Australian brain tries to catch up.

The main cobblestone street in Bourg Saint Maurice is a pedestrianised street, lined with shops for the tourists. There are souvenir shops selling fondue sets, miniature wooden skis, and pretty red and white mugs with love hearts, ready for hot chocolate to be poured into. Then, there is the butcher shop with its beautifully displayed meats (whoever thought a butchers could be so beautiful? There is no other word for it, except gorgeous, impressive, delightful). Then, there is the bakery with its crazy-good croissants, then the tabac shop, then the shoe shops selling mountain boots, and the clothes shops offering ski jackets, beanies, and gloves. Finally, there are restaurants serving typical Savoyard dishes such as tartiflette and fondue. It's all so cosy, so mountain, so fresh. I love it.

It is the weekly market that intrigues me the most, however. It's held on a Sunday and it's a slice of French heaven. I like the market stall sellers. They are jovial, almost clown-like in their manner. They try to draw customers in by making them laugh. Perhaps they are putting on a show because otherwise, their day would be very long. The sellers look like mountain men to me (although most men over 50 years old here look like mountain men to me). They wear jeans, boots, thick winter jackets, and have rugged lines etched into their faces. My imagination likes to think the lines are from all the hard times in the cold climate ushering cows up and down the mountain.

All the usual stalls are here, but I always gravitate to the saucisson stall. I'm always so attracted to the saucisson stall that I wonder if I'm deficient in a certain saucisson mineral or vitamin?

Today, I study the different types of saucisson (what is the English word for saucisson? Is it cured sausage meat? Anyway, the saucissons are long sausages, about 15 centimetres long, with a width of about 2 or 3 centimetres). They sit in hand-woven baskets. The display in this stall looks neat, clean, and inviting. In my opinion, everything in France is about presentation, and of course when it comes to food, also quality, even for saucisson, which is such a basic food. It's pretty easy to make, if you think about it. Mince some meat and fat pieces, stir in some alcohol, add garlic, or herbs, or cheese, or nuts if you like, then knead the mixture by hand, and finally, refrigerate. Next day, squeeze the cool mixture into casings making sure there are no air bubbles, and tie knots at each end. Hang the saucissons in a dry and airy room for a few weeks, and *Voila!*, you've got saucisson. The important thing in the process is that the saucisson needs to have the correct drying environment. A saucisson is going to dry much better at 800 metres altitude than by the sea, and luckily for me and my palate, these majestic Savoyard mountains have plenty of altitude!

'Hello. Would you like to try? This one is the walnut one.' The stall worker offers me a fine slice of his nutty saucisson.

I take the thin slice and look at it. I see pieces of nut inside. I put the slice in my mouth. My eyes roll back. *Mmmmmmmmm!* Who knew I was such a carnivore? I nod to the monsieur, and stroll along the front of his stall, looking at the different baskets. I stroll past the pepper saucisson. I know I would love that one. Then I stroll past the Beaufort cheese one. I think I would like that one, but I'm not too sure about mixing saucisson with good cheese in this format. Is it a waste of good cheese? Then I step past the blueberry saucisson. Again, not too sure. I know I would like it, but I think I'm more of a plain kind of a saucisson girl. Just give me the meat. Or the one with the nuts. It could be a texture thing. Soft cheese bits in the middle of dry hard saucisson doesn't make sense to me. I keep walking, past the garlic one. Yes, I would love that one. I walk past the fennel herb one. Yes, would love that.

Then I get to two baskets that make me stop. The sign above the first hand-woven basket says, 'Sanglier.' I frown. Boar. Boar saucisson. I think, "Well it is wild pig. Probably very good. Have never tried it. Interesting." It's the basket next to it, that makes me really stop still in my tracks. The sign says, "Ane". Donkey saucisson. I frown again, this time more deeply because I think we've crossed a line here. I could not for the life of me think why anyone would want to eat cured minced donkey meat unless times were super bloody hard. My mind races as I stare, and I have to remind myself that food is food. My brains speak to me, "Relax Max, who made you Ms Judgement?" I answer myself. "I did. I made myself Ms Judgement, and I can't look at the Donkey saucisson." I do a u-turn, and go back to the other side of the stall.

'Three for ten euros.' The stall worker smiles at me. The lines etched around his eyes crease. I picture him herding cows up a mountain. I smile, then look down at the baskets, to choose my favourite three. This is going to take a second. Finally, I choose the pepper, the garlic, and the nut one. He was right about giving me the nut one to taste. That was good saucisson.

'Merci.' I hand him my ten euros and take my three saucissons. I smile, careful to walk in the direction away from the Donkey saucisson. I'm such a hypocrite because I eat other animals. Logically, I know I'm being a hypocrite, but it's just the way it is. Donkey is too much for me. Too much. They've gone too far.

5. DELPHINE AND THE HONEY

La Plagne, the Alps, Savoie.

Flora and I carpool to work. One day, Flora drives us in her comfortable new mini. The next day, I drive us in my 1999 green (the kind of green that they no longer use) Fiat Punto that doesn't have Bluetooth or a CD player like Flora's brand new car.

It's 8.01 am. Flora steers along the narrow road and turns up the sound on the radio. Bruno Mars sings out of the speakers, to me. Good morning, Bruno! We approach the first hairpin bend. There are 21 bends to drive past, to get to the resort and our workplace. We work as receptionists for the ski school. We travel up and down this small, windy road each working day. We know each bend, and we know everyone's cars.

Flora looks in the rear-view mirror. 'Look, that's Marco (ski instructor) behind us.'

I point to a white Nissan ahead. 'And that's Jeremy (ski instructor) in front.'

Bruno Mars is still crooning. I sing along because I know the lyrics. French Flora sings the "Oh, oh, oh. Yeah, yeah, yeah" parts. It's a musical workout to get us awake and ready for the day, which will consist of dealing with excited children pre ski lessons, and cold and tired children post ski lessons.

The other morning, on the way up the mountain in the mini, Flora had pointed to the side of the road. 'Look!'

'Oh my God!'

A large deer with large crooked antlers had dashed from the side of the road. He bounced into the forest and disappeared within seconds.

'Wow!' I'd repeated, turning to look back to where he had been.

'*Magnifique!*' Flora had said.

He was *magnifique*. Beautiful, healthy, and elegant. It's not unusual to see wildlife on the road at night. I've seen foxes and young deer, but I've never seen an adult deer like that.

Today, we see a different kind of animal just up ahead; the human kind.

'Look. That's Delphine! I'll stop,' says Flora. She flicks her indicators on, and we pull over.

Delphine is a ski instructor. Something must be wrong with her car because she's hitchhiking up the mountain to get to work. She can't go wrong. There's only one road up the mountain, and one road down the mountain. She knows all the people in the cars going up. They are her fellow ski instructors.

'Good morning, Delphine!' we say.

'Good morning!' Delphine shoots us a big smile as she jumps in the back. 'Thank you.'

'No problem,' says Flora, pulling back onto the mountain road. She turns down the lovely treacle voice of Bruno, and says to Delphine, 'Is your father still doing his honey?'

'Yes! Just put your order in, and I'll bring it. I do a delivery once a week.'

'Honey?' I ask.

Delphine's father keeps beehives, and he collects and sells honey. Quite a few people in the area do the same. I find it interesting. I had never met beekeepers before I moved to this area. A friend of mine, Samuel, does it. I give his kid English lessons, and the teenager entertains me, without realising it. I asked him to use the simple past tense and tell me what he did on the weekend, and the kid said, 'I ate my breakfast. I cleaned my room. And then I went with my father to feed the bees.' His pronunciation is good.

'What do you mean, "feed the bees"?' I'd asked.

'We have to give them food.'

'What food? I thought bees got their own food?'

'Yes, but sometimes there isn't enough food for the bees.'

'So, like... what do you give them? Flowers?'

'No. Water mixed with sugar.'

'And, where are these bees?'

'In the forest.'

'What do you mean, "in the forest"?'

The poor teenager had inhaled at my incessant questions, but he had no choice. 'A little further back, in the forest, we have some hives.'

'Okay. Don't you get scared you'll get bitten?' I pictured the teenager covered in angry bees.

'No. We wear the costume.'

'The white one?'

'Yes.'

'And then?'

'That was Saturday. And then on Sunday, I had to scrape all the honay from the... ' he searched for the word, ' ...from the things. And put them into pots.'

'Honey,' I'd said, correcting his pronunciation.

'Honay,' he'd said, convinced his way was correct.

I'd nodded. Good enough.

'So, Delphine...' I turn around in the front seat to look at Ms Living on the Wild Side/I'll Hitchhike To Work ski instructor, '...how much is your father's honay?'

'My father's honay? (I knew she'd say it like that.) 'Seven euros small pot, twelve euros the big pot.'

'I'll put an order in for next time. Big pot, please.'

Delphine reaches into her bag and writes my name down. 'Okay.'

And, that's the way we do business here in the alps.

A sudden thought. Hey! Maybe this is Delphine's

marketing plan?! She has a whole 20 minutes up the mountain before work, and 20 minutes down the mountain after work, in which to work her "Did you know my family sells honay?" pitch. Clever. Genius really. I like her style, and one week later, I like her direct-from-the-beehive honay.

6. BREAK HIS NUTS

Meribel-Mottaret, the Alps Savoie.

We are in a French ski resort called Meribel. I am a waitress in a hotel which has a ground-floor restaurant.

'He threw a glass at me!' Jelle's blue eyes grow wider and wider.

'What?' I say.

'He threw a glass at me. Nasty motherfucker. I'll kick his fucking nuts!'

Jelle is my work colleague, a fellow waiter. He's 18 years old, and from Amsterdam. He speaks English like he's stepped straight out of the Bronx. I think he's watched a lot of American television.

Guy, the head chef, just threw a glass at Jelle in the kitchen. I don't even raise my eyebrows. Nothing surprises me anymore. It's been drama city since the day I arrived in resort.

The winter hotel staff is a mix of multiple strong personalities. Guy, the head chef, is one of those strong personalities. He hates all the waiters, except for me. I don't condone throwing glasses, but I understand that the chef gets pissed off each winter because he works with a staff that is predominantly English. He calls us *Les Roast Beef*. The waiters, mostly English boarding school boys and very well-mannered, don't know quite what to make of French grumpy Guy. They stay out of his way. But, not my mate, Jelle. Jelle gets in his face. Guy throws a glass at him, and one day Jelle is going to kick his fucking nuts. Apparently.

'I asked the woman at the bar to keep an eye on him,' the hotel manager tells me one day, talking about Guy, the chef.

'Why would you have someone keep an eye on him?'

'He's a very good chef, but he arrives very early at the resort bar each day.'

'What?'

'He's an alcoholic.'

'Ah.' (Well... aren't we all? I am in a very drinky phase at the moment. This is a ski season, after all.)

We all try to stay out of Guy's way. We try to make his life as comfortable as possible, so that he can do his job in peace. And, he does do a good job. The clientele is happy with the food, and the staff is also happy with the food. I have worked jobs before where meals are included in the package, and it's been hit and miss. Here, the staff is fed similarly to the guests. No fondues, raclettes, or steak, and yes, maybe a few lasagnas and spaghetti dishes thrown in once a week, but generally the staff food is very good. It is so good that, weirdly, I am losing weight. I guess living in a mountain can have that effect. There are hills to climb, stairs to walk up, mountains to ski, and frozen lakes to walk around.

My colleagues and I eat before dinner service in the hotel restaurant. It's a chance for the chambermaids, the maintenance guys, the reception staff, and the waiters to come together.

'Bon appétit!' English accents travel around the dining table as we pass the baguettes around.

'Bon appétit!'

'Bon app!'

'I'm bloody starving!'

'Looks good!'

'Dig in!'

Tonight, we are eating a beef dish with a red wine sauce. Baguette bread is perfect for mopping up yummy red wine sauces.

The hotel provides breakfast and dinner for the guests. There is no client lunch service, but the staff lunch is at midday, and it is often the clients' leftovers. Every week, Tartiflette, a traditional dish from the region, is on the hotel menu. It's baked potatoes in a creamy sauce with bacon pieces. It's served with cold meats. The clients get it on Tuesday nights, which means we get it on Wednesdays. Every single week. Not complaining. I think it tastes better the day after.

Breakfast is another story. I've had to cut down on breakfast because between the tartiflette, duck, quail, cheese, and baguettes, it's all become too much. Now at breakfast, I have a little fruit salad and heaps of coffee. When I work the super early breakfast shift starts, I allow myself a *pain au chocolat*, fresh and warm, straight out of the oven.

Despite all the delicious tartiflette, duck, quail, Beaufort cheese, Abondance cheese, Parma ham, and homemade chocolate mousse, many members of the staff are veering more and more towards the alcohol diet. There is a bar at the bottom of the resort, and even though I don't normally drink beer, it is the cheapest drink, so... you know. I've found it drinkable if you put a little banana syrup in it. It sweetens it up. The bar staff knows me as *Demi-Banane*. My two chambermaid work buddies are known as *Demi-Peche* and *Demi-Fraise*. There is no doubt we are all heading further into the alcoholic diet, but... we're not at the Grumpy Glass-Throwing Chef stage... yet!

7. LE QUICHE

Plan d'Eau, Aime, Savoie.

I've been in France long enough to know that if you take a plate of food to someone's house it had better be *fait à la maison,* i.e. made from scratch. By you. At least in my circle of French friends. This poses a problem for me. I grew up in Brisbane and spent a good deal of my childhood in supermarket aisles. I like things in plastic containers, and things you have to rip open. So, the other day when my mates said, 'We're having a picnic at the lake. Everyone bring a dish!' my anxiety started to build. I had seen the types of dishes people bring to picnics. They bring top quality stuff. Shit. The pressure.

Not only do I have a lack of confidence in my cooking skills, I also live in a studio. In my kitchen, there is a mini fridge, a mini freezer, and a mini oven. No excuse, you say? Can still make mini quiches, you say? Yes. Or even one normal-sized quiche. So, I get busy in my kitchen. I studiously look from the computer screen to the bowl in my hand, then back again. I follow the recipe on the screen to a tee, for once in my life, and lo and behold, I am delighted when forty minutes later, I take my quiche out of my mini oven because it actually resembles a quiche. It looks like a real, proper quiche, and it smells very good! Hurrah!

I drive down the mountain, snaking around the 21 hairpin bends, with my quiche next to me, on the front passenger seat. I look across at it after every hairpin bend to make sure it's not sliding. I had tried to put the seatbelt over the quiche, but it didn't stay in place. In the end, I got an old towel out of the boot, and made a little quiche bed for it to snuggle into. At Bend Number 17, I look across again. It's still immobile. Good job.

When I reach the bottom of the mountain, I turn off the road, and follow a long, dirt track surrounded by tall, leafy green trees. I follow the bumpy track until I reach an open clearing where other cars are parked. I take my lovely quiche from its bed, walk across the parking area, cross over train tracks, and continue through the trees till I reach a lake. It is big enough for kids to paddle in, swim in, and play in inflatable dinghy boats in. I shake my head, looking at the water. It's too natural. Too green. Too many weeds. I'm more of a clear blue water girl.

I spot my friends sitting on the opposite side of the barbecue area, far from the children's area with swing sets and rope bridges hanging between trees.

Now, my friends are relaxed and easy people, but let's face it, they are still French. Their food is *always* well-presented. Nicole arrives at the group at the same time as I do. She holds a handwoven basket with a fancy red tea towel draped over it. She places her basket down, and everyone leans forward. She slides the tea towel away to reveal a blueberry tart.

Eyes   glisten   and   noses   sniff.

Mmmmmmmmmmm.'Ooooooooh!'

'Did you make it, Nicole?' Frida asks (as if she had to).

Nicole waves the question away with a casual, 'Oh you know, I went looking for blueberries yesterday and collected enough for this simple tart.'

(Wait a minute. She collected the blueberries herself? In the mountains! I'm still getting used to the fact that blueberries do not originate from supermarkets.)

Frida brought salad. When I think of salad, I think of my favourite salad: lettuce, tomato, onion, feta cheese, and Kalamata olives (I'm addicted to Kalamata olives. Was I Greek in a previous life?). So far with my French friends, I've found salad to mean just lettuce leaves, but Frida's salad is not that. Frida's salad is quinoa, sunflower seeds, pumpkin seeds, lemon juice, lots of other seeds, and crunchy bits of stuff that I don't know what it is.

Laurence stopped off to get fresh baguettes from the bakery, which needless to say are divine, divine, divine.

It comes to my turn. I lay down my tuna quiche covered in the tea towel my Australian next-door neighbour gifted me many years earlier. I pull the old tea towel away to reveal my quiche. Nods of approval travel around my circle of friends. Looking at their expressions, I immediately feel my heart and ego expand. I know that they know that this was an effort for me, and that I had "done good." Phew! And when we eat it later, it is a double phew because it tastes like a real quiche. It is good.

Over the next hour, we eat, talk, and enjoy looking over to the weedy-green lake and the kids playing in it. Further past the lake, amazing snow-capped mountains loom in the distance. It's a very pleasing environment, and a really fun picnic. But, the funniest thing for me is meeting Laurence's boyfriend. He has come down from Paris for the weekend. He is in his mid-forties. He has a nice speaking voice. He asks me what I do. I tell him about my teaching English jobs. Then he says, 'Do you have children?'

'No.'

'Didn't want any?'

Weirdly, and I don't know why I am so open considering I've only just met him, I say, 'I thought I did. I could have sworn I did. But obviously, I had a deeper belief about that within me. Does that make sense?'

He nods.

I look at him and ask. 'And you? What do you do?'

He smiles wryly. 'I'm a psychiatrist.'

I throw my head back and laugh. Willing to leave that conversation there, I reach down, pick up a slice of Nicole's beautiful blueberry tart, and take a bite. Ooooh. I think I can taste the fact that she went hiking up a mountain and hand-selected the best blueberries herself. It's extraordinary. *Mmmmmmmmmmmmm.* It's *délicieux!*

8. *BRAVO ET MERCI*

Peisey, the Alps, Savoie.

The only plant I own lives in Sophie's chalet. Why is my orchid living in my friend's chalet? Because I move back and forth to Paris a lot at the moment. The orchid needs a better caregiver. Sophie is the perfect plant-looker-afterer because she has many of her own. In her large open-plan living room, she walks from plant to plant. She says, 'I can't remember if I told you, but we're going out tonight,'

'Are we?'

'Yes, to celebrate Olivier's medal.'

Olivier is a professional skier, returning from Austria with his medal for downhill skiing.

'The ski club is organising it,' Sophie says.

That night, wearing my beanie that is too big for my head, and rugged up in my puffer jacket and thick snow boots, I stand in the cold air with Sophie, her kids, and all the other people in the village. We have gathered at the bottom of the ski piste. Before long, whispers start to travel through the crowd.

'Here they come!'

'They're coming!'

'Look!'

We turn to see Olivier's mother comes walking through the village with her smiling son, Olivier.

As they reach us, everyone yells, 'Surprise!' Then, we point to the top of the mountain, and suddenly, lights flash on. Blue, red, green, pink, and white lights pop into life. The lights at the top of the mountain start moving in a zigzag down the piste until they get bigger and bigger. Ski instructors and ski patrollers ski in their zigzag, one after the other, carrying the coloured flame torches. My eyes transfix on the beauty of the pretty lights zigzagging down the pure white snow. As I follow the zigzag of lights travelling in the quiet of the night, warmth swirls and swishes around inside me. The skiers arrive one after the other at the bottom of the piste. Finally, the last skier, holding a blue flame, arrives, and everyone breaks into applause. The villagers and I look over to Olivier. I see his eyes glisten with emotion at the local community gesture offered to him. My heart is going to burst right open.

The next part of this surprise celebration is in the community hall. We all walk over to it, and step inside. I notice a long makeshift table to the left. Plates of glorious food decorate the table, but nobody goes to the food, not even the children. Instead, the crowd gathers around the stage area. I follow Sophie to the stage, but my head keeps turning to look back at the food table. My stomach rumbles.

One of the best parts of living in France, for me, is how people eat what I call "the good food" every day. Their "everyday food" is my "special occasion food." This long table in the community hall is lined with "the good food". Hams, olives, fresh bread, salmon, and many varieties of cheese spread across the white tablecloth. The choice of cheese is large: little round cheese, smelly cheese, gooey cheese, and cheese that has been made from the milk of cows who eat certain flowers in a certain area of the mountain. There are even chocolates on the table, and not the kind that come wrapped in plastic or in large blocks. My eyes sweep the table again. I breathe deeply. I am in absolute food heaven.

Standing amongst the crowd, I look at the children. Surely, they must be tempted to go to the food table and ogle the food, no? No. Not one child or teenager even looks at the food table. They are too busy running around and playing.

Suddenly, eight strong men, dressed in jeans, jump on the stage. They wear large black belts around their waist, and attached to each belt is a huge cowbell. Before I know it, the men start rocking their bodies back and forth, and the cowbells ring out. The noise is sudden and deafening. The men ring, and ring, and ring, and ring, and ring, and ring the bells. My hands fly up to cover my ears but I keep my eyes wide open, staring at the heavy bells. I cannot believe cows actually carry these heavy bells, *around their necks*! These can't be the real bells that cows wear? They're too heavy! Surely, these are decoration cowbells? The men continue rocking back and forth on stage, and the room continues to balloon with volume. I look around me at the crowd. Smiles beam on everyone's faces, including the most important person in the room, Olivier. I am deafened by this mountain gesture for one of their own, and touched.

After the cowbell ringing, Olivier takes to the stage to receive his applause and say a few words. His mother looks on from the floor, pride welling in her heart. I glance over to the food table. It is still there. Still no children milling around it. Nobody is even close to it.

At the end of Olivier's speech, everyone bursts into applause. The eight men leave the stage, and the local teenagers run to Olivier, surrounding him and holding up their ski jackets for him to autograph. I look over to the food table. Still nobody.

Finally, ten minutes later, a man stands by the food table and loudly says, 'Please, help yourselves!'

Some people drift toward the food, but most stay chatting in their groups. I look over to the teenagers. They continue milling around Olivier, holding their ski club jackets.

This has got me wondering. What sort of teenager was I? I must have been the greediest girl in Australia, given my recollection of my attitude towards party food.

Looking around this community hall in this small French Alps village, I am once again surprised at how civil people are, when it comes to food.

After another fifteen minutes, my friend, Sophie, says, 'Do you want something to eat? Let's go and get some food.'

I shrug as I turn to look at the food table. My voice is light and lazy. 'Oh, okay.'

9. BARBECUE ON THE TERRACE

La Plagne, the Alps, Savoie.

I've taken a two-month job, teaching English to teenagers at summer camp in the mountain resort of La Plagne. The job sounded so good on paper: teach English in a fun manner in the beautiful alps with clean air. But, show me one kid who wants to learn vocabulary about mountain-biking and horse-riding when the sun is shining and other kids are outside actually mountain-biking and horse-riding.

The job is draining. What can I say? The teenagers are slowly killing me.

Fortunately, the camp food makes up for it. Bless the standard of food in France, because even though this is summer camp where food has to be produced en masse, the standard is good. Quality is always important in France.

The camp dining room is enormous. It looks like any other summer mountain camp dining room except (perhaps) with the exception of our view of the equestrian centre on the left and tennis courts on the right. The wooden terrace leading out from the dining room is just as huge as the inside dining area. Plenty of wooden tables and benches spread across the terrace, each with a large umbrella to provide shade.

Fridays are my favourite day because that's Barbecue Day, where the chefs roll the large black barbecues out onto the terrace, and cook under the hot midday sun. These barbecue meals are not the Australian school barbecue meals I grew up with; that is to say buns, margarine, cheap sausages, cheap hamburger patties, and lots of tomato sauce. These Friday barbecues are all class. Yes, there are sausages, but there is a variety of different herb-flavoured sausages. There is also chicken, skewers of vegetables, and corncobs. Today, the terrace is buzzing with hungry teenagers and hungry camp staff. We must line up to get out meat, then we go inside and top up our plates with salads, and grab some bread (baguette bread, of course. So far, I haven't seen one slice of square white bread at this camp, not even at breakfast).

I like meal times because I sit on the sunny terrace with the activity leaders. My friends are the archery teacher, the dance teacher, the rock climbing teacher, the white water raft guides, and the mountain biking guides. I love the camaraderie.

One of the mountain bike guides comes to sit next to me with his plate of barbecued chicken.

I look at his forearm. It is wrapped in bandages and sits in a sling. 'Oh,' I say.

'Oh.' He half-smiles.

'Bike accident?'

'Stupid bike accident.'

'Ah,' I nod. I look down to his chicken. '*Bon appétit.*'

'Thanks. And you. *Bon appétit.*'

I pick up my knife and my fork, cut my chicken, and lift my fork to my mouth. It's delicious. I glance over to my bike mate from time to time during the course of lunch, and notice he is picking up the easy stuff with a fork in his right hand. He's picking up pasta salad, beans, and tomato. He is not touching the charcoaled chicken. I take a better look at this mountain bike instructor. He's about 30 years old. Blonde, blue eyes, fit. He picks up his tomato piece. I watch him, and start to think, "Is he a guy with an ego? Will he accept my help? His chicken is going cold." After a few more minutes, I can't stand it. I straighten my back and take a deep breath. I point to his plate, and say, 'Would you like me to cut up your chicken for you?'

He smiles and pushes his plate across. I cut his chicken into fork-pinching sizes while he waits. I'm sure he's cursing that last kicker he rode over too fast. Or was it a pebble that brought him down? For the next weeks, he's going to be eating only the easy stuff. I know how he feels because I fell and broke my wrist whilst snowboarding the year before. But, I didn't sit quietly, I asked for help. I saw my next-door neighbour walking towards me in the car park as I headed out for a stroll.

'Hi Jules.'

'Hi Marie.'

'Could you please do me a favour?'

'Yes.'

'Could you please tie up my shoelaces?'

Jules had looked down to my trainers. The laces were

stuffed inside, but not tied. He bent down and did up my laces.

I saw my other neighbour coming up the stairs later on, and shouted, 'François! How are you? Have you got a second to open my jam jar for me? And my olives?'

I used all my neighbours whilst I had a broken wrist.

Back to Summer Camp. He is eating his chicken, and this makes me happy. I look around me. Everyone seems to be happy, enjoying their food in the summer sun. I see 13-year-old Marco, one of my students, laughing with his mates at the table across from us. Marco makes me laugh. The other day, I took my students for what I thought would be a fun English lesson. We went hiking up the mountain and reached a flat part with views overlooking the valley. We took a seat at the sole picnic table on the mountain flat, and the teenagers started talking (in English, that was the rule) about different foods they like. Marco popped out with this doozy: 'I tried monkey brains on pizza. It was good.' He'd nodded, and *the other teenagers nodded too!* Like it was something completely normal! I was too astounded to move. They'd continued on with other things that they like to eat. Not one of them said, "What?! MONKEY BRAINS?!!" I'm still reeling from that little throwaway comment. Either these teenagers are champions at playing things really cool (and playing me), or they are indeed used to, and open to, trying different food.

Today, only chicken and sausages are on the menu, thank goodness, hallelujah, thank you God. And dessert is a choice of a yoghurt, chocolate mousse, or an ice cream.

The teaching is hard work, but the food compensates. And, even better than the food is the lunchtime view to my left. Even with a defective arm, he's easy on the eye.

10. FUN ENGLISH

Macot, the Alps, Savoie.

I have started my own business. I give afternoon tea to French kids, and whilst eating, we do some English speaking. I've called it, 'English Afternoon Tea.' Original, I know.

I have just walked up my steep, narrow road, turned right, walked past the sole bakery in the village, past the adjacent coffee shop/bar where I've only ever seen five people inside at a time, and crossed the street to reach the local school. The Lollypop Man is there. Seeing him makes me chuckle each time because the town is so small. I don't get it because a) he stands at the (one and only) crossing at the traffic lights (cars normally stop at red lights, right?), b) it's a small town of only about 1,600 people, and finally, c) the kids are not stupid (but there's always one right, so I guess, we do need the Lollypop Man). I wave hello to Lollypop Guy and go and wait at the school gates with all the parents. When the teacher opens the gates, gangly kids pile out to greet their parents, but they don't say, 'Hi Mum!' The first words out are, 'What's for *goûter*?' *Goûter* is Afternoon Tea.

My four students come piling out of the gates. I have trained them to say 'Hello' before any question comes out of their ten-year-old mouths. They say it in English, and I reply, 'Hello. How are you?' They reply, 'Fine, thanks.' Then, and only then, are they allowed to revert back into French as we walk back past the bakery, the coffee shop/bar, and turn left into my narrow street. The kids skip ahead of me, each carrying big daypacks on their backs full of really heavy books.

When we get inside my flat, the kids pile their heavy bags in the corner, take their shoes off, and come to stand by the bench in the kitchen. (The taking off the shoes thing always makes me smile. I'm not used to it. I get it with regards to winter because of the snow, but in the summer? But they do it automatically, they're trained. I don't take my shoes off. I'm not trained like that.)

Ten-year-old Arthur sits next to ten-year-old Aurelie, who sits next to nine-year-old Laure. Ten-year-old Stephanie sits at the end of the breakfast bench.

'We had a visit from the nurse today,' says Arthur.

'What did the nurse say?' I ask.

'She told us where babies come from.'

I look up, expecting to see giggling faces, but all I see are nods from Arthur and the three girls. (Why am I the most churlish one?) I push a glass bowl towards them. 'Break the eggs and then mix them in.' I give instructions for the chocolate cake we are making. It's going to cook whilst we practice some English phrases.

Arthur studiously breaks the eggs into the bowl, and the others watch. Each one waits their turn to take the spoon and mix the cake mixture around.

'Put some more flour in,' I say.

'I'll do it!' Stephanie gets the flour and pours. 'This much?'

'Yeah,' I say. Looking over their shoulders, I ask, 'So, where do babies come from?'

Arthur licks his fingers before passing the spoon to Aurelie. 'Well, the bee comes, and he flies over the flower, and he puts his seed in the flower.'

I look at Laure, Aurelie, and Stephanie. They nod in agreement with Arthur.

'Okay,' I say.

The kids mix the batter a little more before lifting the bowl up to me. I look in, and nod. We pour the mixture into the tin, then place it in the oven.

'Can I lick the bowl?' Arthur's big blue eyes look up at me.

I scrunch up my nose. 'That mixture's got raw egg in it.'

'Doesn't matter,' says Arthur, eyeing the bowl.

The kids dip their fingers in. They swipe the side of the bowl and lick the gooey brown mixture. Even Laure.

I give Laure and Aurelie lunchtime English classes. The girls come to my house at midday. We eat lunch, and speak in English. I'm always surprised at how well the girls eat. They are skinny beanpoles but, boy, do they put it away. I offer a main meal and a dessert, which is either a yoghurt or a fruit. Some days, they've had the choice of a chocolate mousse or a plain yoghurt for dessert, and they've chosen the yoghurt. My Australian sugar-addicted brain has never been able to comprehend this.

Ding! Twenty minutes later, in my apartment, the oven bell rings. We stop our English activity and race over to look through the oven glass.

Our faces deflate like the cake in the oven.

'Oh,' says Arthur.

'Oh,' says Aurelie.

'Oh,' says Laure.

'Oh,' says Stephanie.

I say, 'Noooooo!' I open the oven and take out the burnt brown cake with its huge dent in the middle.

Arthur's blue eyes spark up. 'It doesn't matter! It will be okay!'

'You think?'

'Sure!'

'We'll wait ten minutes for it to cool. Come on, let's finish this English game.'

After the game, I say, in French, 'It's cake time. But before we eat the cake, you need to get everything ready. I'm going to give you instructions, in English.'

They listen and try to guess what I mean by Fork, Serviette, Cup, Water, and Plate. They know from previous weeks and also because it's common sense, but I like to think they know because of my teaching.

After the cutlery is in place, we take the dented misery out of the oven, place it on the bench, and cut it up.

Aurelie is the first to take a bite. I look at her face. 'Delicious,' she says.

I don't believe her.

Laure takes a bite. 'Very good.'

I don't believe her.

Stephanie lifts a piece up to her nose, and smells. *Mmmmmmmmm.*

Arthur and I take a bite at the same time. I smile to myself, thinking how trained they are. The way those girls just said, "Delicious. Very good." that wasn't them saying it. That's social norm speaking. That's what we do in France. Manners. Trained behaviour. This cake is a burnt disaster. It's edible, but it has far too much flour, not enough texture, and these polite children are never going to tell me that. Why? Because they train them young here. Food manners. *Vive La France.*

Looking at my cake, I shake my head. It's certainly not my cooking prowess that is going to attract a good bee into my life, that's for sure.

11. LE GRIZZLY

La Plagne, the Alps, Savoie.

The voice on the phone said, 'Hi there. Are you available to work tonight? It's 50 euros.'

For 50 euros cash, I can certainly carry plates. 'Yes, I'll be there.'

That evening, I take the ski gondola up the mountain slope towards the restaurant at the top village. I'm the only one in the cabin and I speak to myself the whole way up. 'Distract. Distract. Distract yourself. The people who make these things know what they are doing. They are professionals. They don't just stick a cabin to a wire in the air and cross their fingers. It's safe. You're safe. It's not like the cabin is going to fall from the sky and crash. Anyway, you would die quickly because of the sudden impact. Or would I? Would it be a slow death? Stop it. Distract, distract, distract.'

Once at the top, I am remarkably still alive. Smiling, I skip over to the chalet-style restaurant.

Inside, it has caramel wooden walls, wooden chairs, and wooden tables. The tables are crammed together, covered with red and white checked tablecloths. The downstairs area is small, with space for about twenty-five people. The upstairs seating area seats thirty-five. You've got to walk up a narrow, squeaky, wooden staircase to get there, and then you need to watch your head because of the slanting roof.

'Thanks for coming in at such short notice!' The owner, a guy in his thirties, smiles at me.

'No problem! Just show me what to do.'

I'm introduced to the main waitress, Elvira, and the work commences. I find it hard to concentrate though because thick juicy steaks with just the right amount of fat keep coming out of the open fire.

The steaks are my first problem.

The second problem is that my hands shake. Not normally, just when I pick up a heavy plate. Do you know how weird it is, to arrive at a table full of hungry, happy guests with their beautiful steak shaking in my hands?

I have willed my hands to stop shaking. I have begged and pleaded with them to stop shaking. I ordered my subconscious to do something about it, but my hands keep shaking. As the night progresses, clients see my shaking hands, and reach up to take the plate from me, but I can't let them. 'Thank you, but the plate is very hot. Please, don't touch it.'

The poor clients must watch me lower the plate onto the table. For them, it's like watching a plane coming into a landing strip in the midst of a typhoon, tilting left and right. The plate wobbles, wobbles, wobbles before eventually sliding into place on the table. Breaths of relief ooze from the clients, and from me.

'Hurrah!' I smile. Oh my God, I'm so drained. Talk about concentration.

As the night goes on, more and more guests see me coming with my shaking hands, a steak in one hand, a risotto in the other. They say things like, 'Don't be nervous. We're not that scary. Promise!'

I have come up with an ingenious response. 'Too much coffee.'

The nods of comprehension go around the table, and my level of embarrassment is somewhat lessened.

This is a lie, of course. I don't drink coffee, for this very reason.

I find a solution. When the chef pushes plates out across the steel counter, I take one plate at a time to the tables, using both hands. No shaking. The tartiflette is posed beautifully on the table. Like a normal waitress.

The fondue is the third problem. I don't want to serve it because it means taking the heavy and chunky fondue set out to the table. Then, you've got to light the bunsen burner thing on the bottom. I'm scared I'll set us all alight.

Elvira sees the worry in my eyes when I call out 'Fondue!' to the kitchen. She says, 'I'll set it up for you. Just tell me when you're ready to take it out.'

'Ah!' The smile on my face is wide. 'Thank you!'

Five hours of work in this cosy mountain restaurant fly by as I continuously seat guests, take orders, serve meals one at a time, clear tables, and reset tables. More people come in for the second wave of the night, and there is hardly a minute to stand still. It's run, race, whoosh, whizz, zoom, and dodge Elvira on the staircase because it's only wide enough for one person at a time. The hours fly by.

There is harmony in this restaurant, between the guests, and more importantly, the staff. It is a good team working here; the owner, two chefs, one dish washer-upper, Elvira, and me. The evening is enjoyable. It's just a pity I have the shaky shaky shaky thing going on. I know I won't take an offer of working here again, despite the agreeable environment. My shaking hands are against me. I make a decision. No more waitressing for me. However, starting tomorrow, I will pick up hand weights, and begin strengthening my wrists. There is no way I'm heading for a future of the shakes! Yes to a future of juicy steaks, though. Hey... maybe steaks will cure the shakes? Maybe I need more iron?! I think I'm onto something!

12. I SEE SOMETHING

La Plagne, the Alps, Savoie.

Sophie's mother and father live up the mountain in a big, two-storey chalet set on a large piece of land. The chalet looks over the side of the mountain, and down into the valley. I often see Sophie's parents in their garden when I'm driving past, on my way up the mountain to my place. They have a cherry tree out the front, with a plastic table and chairs under it. It's an idyllic mountain setting. Along the side of their chalet, cut-up pieces of logs line the wall, for their wood fire. At the back, they have a large vegetable patch. Whenever Sophie's mother, Sandrine, arrives at her daughter's home, she always comes with food from the vegetable garden and fruit trees in her hand.

She says, 'This is a jam I made from the strawberries. We had so many strawberries!'

or

'This is saucisson your father made.'

or

'This is a courgette conserve.'

Sandrine is elegant, with a good figure. I think it's a mix of good genes plus a good regime. She eats good quality food that she and her husband have grown.

Sophie and I travel up the mountain this night, with Sophie's two teenage daughters in the back seat. The mountain road consists of one narrow lane for cars going up, and one narrow lane for cars going down. It is unlit and surrounded by lush forest on either side.

My friend, Isa, said to me once, 'Be careful on the drive home, Marie. It's dangerous at night. Animals cross the road. Always look out for yellow eyes ahead.'

I point to the trees by the side of the road, and say to Sophie, 'I saw a deer the other day. He was superb, with huge horns.'

'Lucky you. Yes, there are lots of deer. Madeleine (her neighbour) gets them in her garden at night.'

'Wow!' I say. 'Do you know what I haven't seen yet?'

'What?'

'Boar. Have you seen boar when you've been driving?'

'No. But my aunt gets them in her garden at night. She can't see them, but she hears them snuffling and grunting.'

We travel up the mountain road, past 15 hairpin bends, and finally pull into her parents' chalet driveway. Sandrine and Phillipe are waiting for us, ready to celebrate their granddaughter's birthday. They give us two kisses hello on each cheek. Sophie's cousins have already arrived, and greet us in the living room when we get inside. After introductions are made and kisses hello are given, we settle at the kitchen table for nibbles.

When the main course arrives, it is a meat dish. The salad (only lettuce leaves) is served after the meat dish, as a separate dish. It   is served with Sandrine's homemade vinaigrette.

Sandrine has spent years working in a restaurant higher up on the mountain, where there is no road access. They had to use a ski mobile with a trailer to deliver groceries to the restaurant. After so many years in the restaurant business, serving food comes as second nature to Sandrine. After the main meal, in a most professional manner, she presents the birthday cakes.

I've come to realise with this family that their desserts always come in pairs. There are always two cakes, and everyone always has a slice of each. It's not a choice of one or the other. Tonight, we have an apple tart, plus a strawberry and cream cake. All eyes go to the strawberry and fresh cream cake.

Sophie's father, distracted by outside, points to the large kitchen window. He says, 'There was a herd of deer grazing up there last night.'

I look out at the large space of land backing away from their chalet. In the distance, I see the beginning of the thick forest which leads all the way up the mountain. 'Wow!'

'We see a lot of animals here.'

I keep looking out the window. I think I see something in the night. I squint my eyes. 'Is that... ?'

Everyone looks.

A smile spreads over my face as I'm convinced I see my

favourite mountain animal, the marmot. In my intermediate French, and with my Australian accent, my words come out as, 'Is that, is that, is that... a mammoth?'

'A mammoth?' All eyes definitely look out the window.

I nod. 'Yes! I think it is!'

'Where?!'

I point to the sloping piece of land. 'There!'

Laughter rips around the table. 'Where?! Where is the mammoth?!'

I don't get it. I don't get their sudden laughter. I point, again. 'There!'

All throughout the course of dessert, I endure the cousins and the teenagers mimicking my accent. "I think I see a mammoth!" I make a mental note to work on my pronunciation skills. I've already begun practising in my head. *Marmotte. Mammouth (prononced marmoot). Marmotte. Mammouth.*

The strawberry and cream cake is dynamite. The sponge is fresh and fluffy; the cream has just the right amount of sweetness, and the strawberries from the garden are ripe and juicy. Lily, the birthday girl, beams.

At the end of the night, goodbye kisses are given on both cheeks. Sophie, myself, and the girls pile into the car, and Sophie drives slowly down the mountain. There are no other cars on the windy road, and there are no street lights. It's complete darkness.

I sit in my front passenger seat. 'Wow, that strawberry cake was something else!'

'Yes. She knows it's Lily's favourite.'

'Mine too, now.'

'Yes, everyone loves that cake.'

Sophie suddenly slams on the brakes. We jolt forward in our seats. The headlights illuminate the road ahead. A thick boar with gristly fur trots across the road in front of our eyes.

Sophie and I look at each other. Our jaws drop, then we burst out laughing at the same time. 'HA HA HAAAAAAAAA!'

I forget there are kids in the back seat, and scream, 'No fucking way! We were just saying!'

Sophie and I get into a fit of laughter. 'Ha ha ha! Ha ha ha!'

We can't stop.

'Ha ha ha! Ha ha ha!'

Eventually, Sophie calms down enough to restart the car, and we continue down the mountain, with full tummies and happy souls. We saw the rare boar tonight, and in my mind, the even more rare, in fact no longer existent, mammoth.

13. MARRIOTT BUSINESS ENGLISH

14th arrondissement, Paris.

It's been several weeks now that I have been walking into the Hotel Marriott in Paris the 14th. The hotel sits on a wide boulevard that is very pleasant to walk along because it is tree-lined. I remember Audrey's first phone call to discuss our English lessons.

'Meet me at the Hotel Marriott in the 14th?'

Holding the phone to my ear, I had raised my eyebrows. 'The Marriott?'

'Yes. It's just near my work, and they have a restaurant.'

Still with raised eyebrows, I'd nodded slowly. 'Okay. We'll meet there.'

I was surprised at her choice, but the Hotel Marriott turns out to be a good place to give English lessons in. It's much less busy and noisy than if we had have met in a "normal restaurant." The ambiance is business-like, and the decor is elegant and welcoming. The seats are spacious, cushiony, and bright; orange or lime. Little, low, round tables stand between the chairs, and each table is spaced out, unlike "normal restaurant" tables.

They sell Starbucks coffee in the Marriott. Not that I drink coffee these days, but, hey! Starbucks inside the hotel! Catering to international people. Not bad, not bad.

Today, I have arrived, and am sitting towards the back, waiting for Audrey. She is at the takeaway section of the restaurant. There is the fancy part of the restaurant, the part where they serve you at your table, and then there is the less fancy part where they have pre-prepared food and the coffee bar (Starbucks). Audrey always goes to the Starbucks part to get her food before coming to sit with me. I don't eat during our lessons because I'm teaching.

Whilst waiting for Audrey, I sit on my cushiony, lime chair and look up to see a very tall man to my right. I frown because another very tall man stands next to him. These men are not the usual tall. There's something different. Then, I notice a photographer. My eyes move across, past the photographer, and I see a whole group of very tall men. I'm proud of the fact that I even notice, because I can be the most unobservant person in the world at times (which is weird considering I'm also a comedian). Yet, today, I make the connection. This is a basketball team doing some promotion. Which basketball team, who knows? But, and I don't know why, I like the fact these tall, fit men are standing within my proximity. Ooooh.... celebrity!

Audrey walks over to me with her tray of food, nonplussed by the basketballers. I see she's chosen a vegetable soup, a chicken quiche, and a little chocolate cake. We have the conversation I've been dying to have with a French working person for ages.

'If I may ask, Audrey, how is it that most French people eat at restaurants each lunchtime? For me, eating in a restaurant is a luxury, it's something special. I'm used to taking my own lunch to work, eating it in the staff room, or in the park, or at my desk. How can so many French people afford to eat three-course meals each day?'

'We have restaurant tickets. It's part of our salary package. The government subsidises it. So, say the meal costs ten euros... I buy the tickets for five euros from my workplace, and my workplace pays five euros. So this meal,' she points to her soup, quiche, and chocolate mousse, 'only cost me five euros really, but it sells for ten euros. Everyone does it like that.' She continues, 'Some people do bring their lunch and eat in the staff room. There is a microwave, but most of my colleagues eat out each day.'

I nod, fascinated with the culture. I see it every midday. Teams of employees stream out of office buildings and head to restaurants, to eat hot meals. Of course, my Australian mind associates restaurants with taking your time, having large portions, and being too full at the end. But here, from what I've seen, three-course lunchtime meals are medium-sized, and the dessert is small; a token dessert if you will. Everything seems balanced. I look at Audrey's tray. I think I would still be hungry after the soup, quiche, and chocolate mousse.

Audrey and I have eaten in a "normal restaurant" at other English lessons (she's eaten, I've taught). So, I've seen her eat bigger portions than the Marriott takeaway food, but she always has three courses. It never wavers. And she always finishes everything. This woman is short and thin. I shake my head. After years of living in France, it still befuddles me.

The "sit down and eat a proper hot meal" is in Audrey's

psyche. It wouldn't occur to her to grab a hotdog on the street, or a sandwich, not unless she was very restricted with time. This mentality of the three-course sit-down meal starts at a young age, as soon as the kids go to school. They eat lunch together in the canteen. Even in kindergarten, it is three courses. The kids are encouraged to try everything.

My friend Sophie told me once, 'In Loane's school (Loane is four years old), the kids are not allowed to *not* eat the food. If they say, "I don't like it," they must at least take a bite to try it, *then* if they don't like it, they are allowed to not eat it, but they must try it." I'd raised my eyebrows imagining little four-year-olds picking up saucisson and biting into it. Sophie continued, 'Today they gave them Abondance cheese to try. They give them different cheese all the time.' I'd nodded, impressed.

Sitting here with Audrey, I look around the Marriott. The basketballers have moved on. Businessmen, businesswomen, and holidaymakers are enjoying their three-course meals. It is so civilised. I like it. I like the three-course meal. I'm a language teacher, teaching clients at their workplace normally. My hours are dependent on the client. I don't have restaurant coupons, and I don't have colleagues to sit with and eat at lunchtime. But, I want to. I want to eat in a restaurant every day of the damn week. This is my dream! And if I could just get rid of the "I could never afford it" attitude ingrained in me, I might just get there one day. When I do, I'll order two desserts if necessary (Oooh, I say that, but I know I wouldn't. In France, that's not done. We conform. We conform. We conform.)

14. JAM CREPES

Porte De Clignancourt, Paris.

'Madame! Look. Look. Look. Look. Look. Look.' The man follows me as I walk towards the famous *Clignancourt* flea markets, *les marchés aux puces*.

I had gotten out of the Porte De Clignancourt Metro, walked past KFC on the corner, past the discount sports shoe shop, past the cheap mobile phone shop, and past the kebab place. Then, I'd crossed the little street, and now I am walking along the stretch of road heading to the ring road and the flea markets. Men stand along this wide stretch of footpath, selling random things that they hold in their hands. They hold perfume, beads, necklaces, packets of shirts, and underwear. The guy I'm currently walking past holds Top Gun-style sunglasses. I'd made the stupid mistake of glancing at the sunglasses.

The man saw my glance and he launched into sell mode. 'Madame! Look. Look. Look. Look. Look. Look.'

I walk past him, his grey hair, and his thick, grey

moustache, but he is intent on getting me to buy. He walks alongside me, keeping the same pace as me. Luckily for me, I'm feeling good today. I'm feeling strong, and as always when I walk the streets of Paris, I've got my music in my ears, hands in my pockets, and sunglasses on. That's right. I have my own sunglasses. I don't need Top Gun.

But the man follows me. 'Look. Look. Look. Look. Look. Look. Look. Look.'

Apart from that one glance to the glasses, I haven't looked anywhere but straight ahead. Hands in pockets. Earphones in ears. Eyes straight ahead. The body language could not be more clear. I continue. The man continues alongside. We walk past a dude with chocolate in his hands, past a dude with cigarettes in his hands, past a dude with earrings, and past a dude with men's cologne. Moustache Man continues to walk alongside me, with his sunglasses in his hands. 'Look, look, look, look, look, look, look.' He is stubborn. But guess who is more stubborn? Me. I walk, looking straight ahead, and never acknowledge him even though he is right at my side, and trust me, I'm walking calmy, at quite a slow pace. I am not going to scurry away. He continues alongside me. We're nearly at the ring road. 'Look. Look. Look. Look. Look. Look. Look. Look.'

I chuckle internally. How screwed up are things, that I am taking mild enjoyment from not looking at the man? It's because I find these guys so annoying and so heavy. For once, I am being the heavy one, and I like that I am giving him a taste of some sort of medicine. I feel the other street vendors watching Moustache Man. They see he is getting more and more desperate. That's the best part.

Finally, Moustache Man breaks. He lowers his hands, and says, 'You're not even going to look?'

I'm not going to look, Dude. I'm on a food mission. I keep walking, slowly and surely, towards the flea markets.

The guy falls away. He must walk back past the other street vendors, walking his "no-sell walk of shame."

I cross the street, walk under the large ring road overpass. This section smells of urine. I cross the street and arrive at the markets. I came to these flea markets a couple of weeks ago, looking for trainers. I found the prices were higher than expected. I actually found cheaper trainers in the shop near KFC. So, two weeks ago, I hadn't found the shoes I wanted, but I had discovered, amongst the clothes, perfume, antiques, records, and phone accessories stalls, that there are some fabulous food stalls. A caravan selling crêpes for one euro fifty had gotten my attention. A jam crêpe for one euro fifty?! That's my type of crêpe!! I had seen other stalls selling crêpes, but none at one euro fifty. I didn't buy two weeks ago; I hadn't had change on me. Today, I'm rich. I've got three euros (because I know myself, but we'll start with one first).

I continue along. My eyes glance at the shoe display and straight away, the young, thin guy is on it.

He calls to me as I walk, 'Madame! Madame! Look!'

I don't look. I might be the only person who comes to the flea market to not look. I come to eat. Up ahead, I see it. The white caravan with the one euro fifty crêpes. I feel around in my pocket to make sure my purse is still there. It is. In the food caravan. A woman, about 50 years old with auburn hair tied up in a ponytail, stands spreading crêpe mixture over a round hot plate. She moves the yellow mixture around and around like a professional. I think she's been working in this caravan all her life.

'Nutella?' Red Ponytail asks the waiting customer.

'Yes.' The man stands, with his coins in his hands, eyes on the crêpe.

Fudge sit in little piles at the front display. On the left side of the caravan, a rectangular whiteboard hangs.

Crêpe confiture 1€50

Crêpe citron sucre 2€

Crêpe Nutella 3€

Red Ponytail looks at me. *'Madame?'*

'Une crêpe confiture, s'il vous plait.'

'Abricot ou Fraise?'

'Fraise, s'il vous plait.'

She spreads the yellow mixture over the round hotplate. I have been dreaming about this for two weeks and here we are, my dream is coming true! She flips my crêpe and spreads red jam over it. When it's ready, she folds the crêpe into four, and slips it onto a waxy piece of paper. She says, *'Un euro cinquante.'*

Smiling, I hand over my coins.

Walking away through the crowds with my hot crêpe in my hand, I lean forward and smell it. Oooooh, good. I take the first bite. My eyes flutter. Perfect. Sweet and hot. I know there and then, that after I've done the tour of the markets and been harassed by men calling me to look, I will be back for another crêpe to fortify me on my walk back to the Metro past the street sellers and Moustache Man. I take another bite of my piping hot crêpe. *Mmmmmmm.* If only you could see me now. Look look look look look look look look look.

15. PARISIAN LUNCH SERVICE

Le Marais, 3rd arrondissement, Paris.

I hadn't seen my Australian friend, Rachel, in 30 years. The last time I saw her, we were both wearing olive green dresses, brown shoes, brown socks, and saying "yes" to the nuns at the Catholic convent high school. Thank God, things have changed! He, he, he.

Thirty years later, we met up in Lyon, during a break from a boat tour Rachel and her husband were enjoying. She had contacted me saying she would be in Lyon on this particular date, and would I be free. I was. And when we met up, something magical happened. Even though we weren't in the same group of friends in high school, here, in Lyon, we truly gravitated to the other. We talked, laughed, bonded, and discovered the other. Warm vibes bounced between us.

We maintained contact since that day, and thanks to her husband's job, Rachel is back in France this year, in Paris. I am also in Paris this year! Yippee!

Rachel messaged me the other day. 'We're staying in the *Le Marais*. Can you meet me outside the Metro St Paul?'

'Sure!'

'We'll have lunch in one of the restaurants nearby.'

'Can't wait!'

My heart races. Today is the day I am meeting Rachel for the second time in 31 years. I have decided to wear jeans and a loose, white, cotton top. It's August, and Paris is hot and sticky. I get off the Metro, race up the stairs and into the sunlight. There she is, wearing her classy, orthopaedic-can-walk-on-cobblestone-streets-all-day shoes, and a big smile.

'Squeeeeeeeeeeeeeeeeeeeeee!' I hug her tightly. 'You look fantastic!'

'And you!'

'I can't believe it!'

'Me neither!'

'Ha ha ha!' I link arms with her. 'Come on. Let's find a place to eat, so we can sit and chat!'

She points across the road, towards the centre of *Le Marais* quarter. 'I saw some restaurants in the little streets this way.'

The streets are cobbled (I live in sneakers for this reason) and narrow. Lots of beautiful old buildings, and lots of cute restaurants. We come across one that has dollhouse-like square tables on the footpath. The front of the restaurant displays a yellow banner with white lettering. Inside, it looks small and cute.

'Here?' Rachel asks.

'Yes!'

We step inside to see if we can get a table on the footpath. The waiter is very busy. Looks like he's working on his own.

I say, in French, 'Hello. A table for two?'

He nods as he's picking up menus. He says, in English. 'Yes. Take a seat.' He is that busy that he doesn't even look at us.

I'm not impressed. I say, in French, 'Can we sit on the terrace?'

He says, in English, 'Yes, I'll be out.' He still doesn't make eye contact, and skips past us to go outside.

This is not good. The dude has done what I hate the most. He has spoken to me in English after I spoke to him in French. It's my pet peeve because I have made such an effort to get my French up to scratch. This only happens with younger generation waiters. I rarely experience this in other French cities, but in Paris, waiters speaking back to me in English happens so often that I have come to believe they see me as an opportunity to practice their English. My French friends will argue that they are just trying to make my life easier, that waiters often have people stumbling along in French, so to quicken up the process, they just speak in English. I'm calling this as bullshit because my level of French is good. You don't need to help me. I've done the work. *Je parle français.*

We take a seat outside. Rachel is happy because the restaurant is really cute. I look at the menu, then I look back to the skinny waiter running around. My nose scrunches up. Then, my lips purse. 'No. Let's go. I'm not feeling it.'

My friend's happy eyes suddenly widen. 'What?'

I'm already on my feet. 'No. We're not eating here. He's rude.' I walk off.

Rachel follows me around the corner, where, fortunately, loads more restaurants line the street. We stop at one that has a spare table for two on the footpath. A blackboard by the front door lists their lunchtime formula: three courses for 18 euros. Rachel looks at me with expectant eyes. I smile.

The waiter comes out, makes eye contact, smiles, and says, 'Can I help you?'

'A table for two, please? This one?' I say, in French, pointing to the table on the footpath.

Smiling, he looks me in the eye, and replies (in French), 'Yes, please take a seat. I'll be out with the menus.'

Aaaaaaaaaaaaaaaaaaaaaagh! Friendly customer service in *Le Marais*! It's our lucky day! Happy, happy, happy me. Relieved, relieved, relieved Rachel.

The restaurant is a good choice. We had a salad for starter, but it is the main meal that did it for me. It was mackerel with vegetables. It was cooked well, in a lot of butter. The dessert is a café gourmand; it's an expresso coffee with an array of mini desserts. There is a mini chocolate mousse, a meringue, a biscuit, and a mini custard tart. I am not impressed with the café gourmand, but the fish main course was excellent.

This is a funky little restaurant. Before the first course arrived, we'd dashed inside to the Ladies room on the first floor. It was empty, and we looked around, spinning out at the funky purple wallpaper and yellow velvet chaise longue sofas. We had an impromptu photo session, sprawling out on the kitsch sofas.

Back downstairs on the busy little footpath-acting-as-a-terrace, I look around at the other guests, enjoying their three-course meals. I inhale a long, happy breath. I love eating in restaurants in France. There is such an array. There is no reason why one should not have a good quality experience, *and* smiling, helpful service from the waiter. *Non?*

16. BARBES MILLE-FEUILLE

18th arrondissement, château Rouge, Paris.

I like *mille-feuilles*. A mille-feuille is a rectangular pastry of three layers. The bottom and middle layers have custard between them, and the top is covered in icing. A custard slice, if you will.

There is a bakery in the 18th *arrondissement* on the corner near the comedy club I gig at. It's nothing spectacular, but it always looks clean and fresh. I regularly drool at their selection of pastries on my way to my gigs.

So, it's Sunday night. I'm putting on my make-up because I'm about to go out to do a gig, and instead of thinking about my set and what I'm going to say to the audience, I'm thinking about the mille-feuille. As I apply my mascara, I say to myself, 'You do this gig, and as a reward, if the bakery is still open when you finish, you buy one of those mille-feuilles. And you eat it without any guilt.' I nod in the mirror. Deal done.

Dolled up and ready to be funny, I step out the door,

walk five minutes to the metro station, and take the train across town to château Rouge station. It's then a four-minute walk from the metro to the comedy club but wow, those four minutes are full of everything. Like, *everything*. As I walk, I've got my head slightly down. I mind my own business because there is enough business already going on in this street. There's the legit business, and there's the less legit.

It's 8 pm. The stores are still open. I walk past the butchers. This butcher does it savage style. The focus of this butcher is certainly not on presentation. Presentation has been flung out the window, and what's been flung in, is big fat fresh meat chunks. Meat chunks have been thrown over each other, and they pile up amongst goats' heads and pigs' hooves. Raw meat spreads out everywhere. I'm fascinated, but distracted at the same time, because there is a lot of other street stuff happening simultaneously. There is a dude selling peanuts off of a plastic sheet on floor, there are older African women selling drinks out of their nana trolleys, and there are prostitutes standing by. A lot of hustle and bustle here. People are coming and going, coming and going, coming and going. I shuffle through. I pass the small African food stores with plantains out the front, past the hair product stores, and past the mobile phone shop. I'm coming up to the bakery, but I stop at a restaurant just before it. When I say *restaurant*... well... it looks a bit makeshift. I stare at the window display. The display is like the neighbourhood; there's a bit of everything going on. There's Chinese rice, Chinese beef, then shoved in the middle are African-style whole fried fish, then some Chinese Chicken, then some sardines. I stare at the whole fish. I want one. Two, maybe three. I keep walking to the corner. I glance, yep, the mille-feuilles are there. I smile. Good, I will get one tonight, provided we finish early enough. Sometimes the club closes really late and we race to get out for the last metro home at 12.45 (which is when the business on this street *really* comes to life. Busy, busy, busy.)

I feel my pocket for my purse. I have about five euros in change. Enough to get a mille-feuille and maybe, maybe, maybe something else. Cause I'm greedy. And, it's not that the mille-feuilles in this place aren't a decent size. They're great. They're Australian-size. I salivate.

Inside the comedy club, with their drinks and peanuts on little round tables, the audience sits up, eager to be entertained. Tonight, I share the bill with 7 other comics. We do 8 minutes each on stage, make the crowd laugh, and then, just like that, the show is over.

Downstairs in the dressing room, I check the clock. We have finished on time, which is good because there is another show on straight after ours.

I wave to the other comedians. 'Goodnight. Thank you. Good Gig.' A couple of them have ordered hamburgers and fries from the club and are hoeing in. The burgers look fresh. *'Bon appetit!'* I say as I hurry out of the club. I look to the corner ahead. The lights are on! Excellent! At the corner, I push the door open and my eyes go to the mille-feuilles. There is one left! There are two people in the queue before me. I start to pray. 'Please God, don't let them take my mille-feuille. You know how long I've been fantasising about this.' My eyes scan the rest of the pastries in preparation for Plan B.

It's the end of the evening, and there is not much left, just the usual suspects: *a couple of chausson aux pommes*, three *Religeuses*, one chocolate slice, three strawberry and cream slices, some *pain aux raisons*, and a couple of *pain au chocolat* that look deflated and sad. Then, I spot something that I don't usually see in bakeries. Jam Donuts. The English kind. (I don't know if these donuts are English, I just associate them with London because I ate them a lot there. They are the round ones without the gaping hole, just a little hole where the baker squeezes jam inside. These ones here are jumbo size. Goooooooooooood.)

The server calls me forward. *'Madame?'*

I look back to the glass pane. I send up a silent thank you to the sugar gods. *'Une mille-feuille, s'il vous plait.'*

'Anything else?'

I bite my bottom lip. I squint. 'And a jam donut, please.'

'Strawberry, apple, or apricot?'

I want strawberry, but for some ridiculous reason I say, 'Apple.' I tell myself apple is healthier. It will balance everything out.

It is a 30-minute trip home on the metro, and then a five-minute walk from the metro to my place. All through the trip, I manage to protect my pastries, sheltering them from bumping into anything. They are as precious as newborn babies. I get back to my tiny studio that doesn't even have its own toilet. I have to share a toilet with the three neighbouring studios. I can't believe I am living like this. I'm an adult, for goodness sake.

I boil the water for my tea, and I sit at the little table that folds down from the wall. It's past midnight. I remind myself of the deal I made in the mirror before I left tonight. No guilt. I lay out my feast. I take a bite of the mille-feuille. It's brilliant. It's better than brilliant. It fulfills all my expectations. I am so happy and appreciate each bite. Then, I look at the jam donut. I could leave it for tomorrow. I'm not hungry now. I pick it up. I take a bite. I'm disappointed with the apple. The filling is not sweet enough, but it doesn't matter because the dough and the sugar are good enough to carry it. I eat the whole donut. By the time I finish both pastries, I am buzzing. I have a sudden urge to put my running shoes on and zip, zip, zip away! I want to run all over Paris. But it is one o'clock in the morning. I'm an addict. I've had my dose of stage adrenalin, and my sugar hit. Now I need to come down by staring at stupid stuff on the internet till I feel sleepy enough to go to bed. I don't think it works like that. Doesn't matter. Sugar, sugar, good.

17. FOOD CAMP

La Courneuve, Paris.

I step out of the metro at La Courneuve 8 Mai 1945. It's at the end of the pink line. They had said, 'Be careful when walking from the metro to the place. The neighbourhood can be a bit rough. Just watch your stuff.'

As I walk the metro corridor towards the exit, I see it. Guys stand around in twos and threes. I can't hear what they're saying, but their body language tells me stuff is going on. I keep walking.

Outside the metro station, the ground is barren. I walk towards a low building standing on its own on the block of dry land. The building is fenced off with barbed-wire fencing. A group stands at the entrance, and I go to join them.

A tall woman with red hair, pale skin, and dressed in what I call "Not-French clothes" soon comes and stands next to me. She is about my age. I smile. She smiles. She says, *'Bonjour tout le monde!'* with a great big happy smile and a great big foreign accent.

I say to her in French, 'My name's Marie. Where are you from?'

'Australie!' she says with flourish.

'Me too.'

She switches to English. 'No way! I'm from Brisbane. You?'

'Me too!' I smile.

She shakes her head. She loudly says, in French, to the other people, whom I don't know, and I'm pretty sure she doesn't know, 'She's from Australia! Like me!'

The people nod politely, then go back to staring at the fence.

Soon, a person wearing a thick blue ribbon necklace with a badge comes walking to the fence. He unlocks the gate, and we file in. 'Go straight ahead. It's the second door on the left.'

Our group walks into a huge hall lit by fluorescent tubes. Lots of tables, the types that have metal legs and can be folded up and down, are set up for dining.

'Have you volunteered here before?' asks Donna, my new Australian friend.

I shake my head.

Donna leans in close, and whispers, 'I have. They're a pretty dry bunch, let me tell you.' Then, she lifts her head, smiles, and shouts (in French), 'Happy to be here! Nice to be back! Good to see you!'

The other volunteers smile politely.

I have been in France long enough to be able to read certain things correctly and I think I'm reading it correctly when I say that they are simply being French by not responding with the joy which Donna is trying to provoke. I also think I'm correct in saying that Donna is simply being Australian with her open, for-everyone-to-see happiness. Ah, culture differences. I chuckle to myself.

A woman from the kitchen area comes over to me. 'Marie, can you please fold the cutlery into these paper serviettes? And make a pile on this tray. We don't have a lot of time. Doors open at 7 pm.'

I nod.

Donna is assigned the same job. We stand side by side, and wrap forks, knives, and spoons into paper serviettes.

The other volunteers, standing further along by the serving tables, are welcoming, but very occupied. There is a lot to do before the doors open. They seem to know each other, and they each have their particular tasks to complete. They get to work. I am impressed by the production. I watch them set up the food on makeshift tables, lined side by side to make one long table. On the first table, there is a large bowl of tomato and pasta shell soup. Further along, there is fruit. Then, there is yoghurt. Then, the bottled water, and lastly, the bread table. A volunteer is busy cutting up baguettes. I stare at the mountain of bread. Wow, loads and loads of bread.

'Marie, you will be in charge of the fruit tonight.' A young volunteer calls me over to the "fruit table" to show me where I am to stand. She points to two crates of fruit on the table. One is full of bananas, and the other one is full of apples. Both look dire. The bananas are half yellow half black, and the apples are not that much better. I'm surprised because the food on the other tables looks copious and of good quality, but the fruit...

'You go through, and throw out any fruit that is not good, and put it in this bucket. Okay?' says the young volunteer. I think she is the supervisor.

I nod. I pick up the first unfortunate-looking banana and go to put it in the bucket.

'No, that one is good.' she says. She takes my banana and puts it back in the crate.

'Oh?'

'Yes. It is okay. Just the ones that are really bad.'

I nod, but I think, "Shit!"

'And they only get one fruit. Either a banana or an apple. Not both. Okay?'

I nod, but I think, "Shit!"

Donna gets assigned to the table next to me. She is to distribute the yoghurts.

Under the makeshift tables, I see there are more pots of yoghurt, and more crates of unfortunate fruit.

At 7 pm on the dot, the doors open, and a line of men stroll forward in a queue. They grab a tray, and make their way across our line, collecting their soup, fruit, yoghurt, bread, and water bottle. They greet the volunteers in low voices, and the volunteers smile and return their greetings in quiet, low voices.

Not Donna.

'Bon appétit!' she yells, smiling as she places a yoghurt on the person's tray.

I chuckle. Even the refugees don't know how to take her. Most smile, and a few do the same chuckle that I did. I see they appreciate her joviality.

'Strawberry or peach? Which one?' Donna calls in her loud voice. 'Here you go, young man!' She places a pot of yoghurt onto the guy's tray.

Meanwhile, I try to give away my half-yellow half-black bananas, but nobody is taking them. I don't blame them. They choose the wonky apples instead. Soon, however, I have a situation. A man, with his tray of soup, arrives, and points to the banana crate. I give him the very best one I can find, but then he points to the crate again. I look to see if my supervisor is around. She is not looking, and I give him the second-best banana I can find.

The line moves quickly, and soon the dining room is full of men of all different ages. I'm surprised (I don't know why) that there are a lot of young guys. Everyone is polite. It is a pretty sombre experience for me. These men are in a position that no one wants to be in. They graciously accept the food, but it's obvious they do not want to be in this position. There is a certain solemnness to the queue.

I see only two women amongst all the men in the queue. They look rough. They stand out, and they also stand their ground. They talk loudly, over all the men.

As the men, and two women, take their seats at tables with other men that they don't know, the room soon fills with noise.

'No. Only one,' says the volunteer at the end table, when a man in the queue asks for more bread. 'After, when everyone is finished, and if there is still more bread left, then you can have it.'

I shake my head. There is a mountain of bread. It's ridiculous how much bread there is. Just give him the bread. Fuck.

My supervisor comes past. She notices I have replaced the wonky apple crate with a new fruit crate. This time it's oranges. Again, these are not the oranges you see on display at Monoprix supermarket. These are the rejects of the rejects. But, they probably taste just as good. 'Everything okay, Marie?' she asks with a smile.

I ask about the bread. 'It looks very good. Where does it all come from?'

'From the bakery school. Every evening they donate what they have made.'

I see that next to the baguette bread there is a fruity type bread. 'Oh, that is excellent,' I say.

'Yes, it is a good organisation. We are lucky to be able to do this every day.'

I agree. It is a well-run organisation, even if a little mean with the bread distribution. Maybe that volunteer is scared of being told off? France can quite be scholarly, let's say.

My Australian colleague continues to shout over everyone in her loud accent all night, and the more she shouts, the more the French retreat. I continue chuckling.

At the end of the night, Donna whispers to me, 'And you watch... These guys are so stingy, they won't even offer us a bowl of soup at the end.'

I had wondered about that. And she is right. But I don't

complain. I am surprised though. I had eyed that fruity bread all evening. Would have loved a big chunk. I chuckle resignedly to myself as I sweep the floor at the end of the night when the men have left (to sleep I don't know where), and the hall is empty.

Donna comes over with her coat. 'When you're ready, grab your coat. We'll go back to the metro together. It's not good to walk on your own.'

I grab my coat, wave, smile, and say goodnight to everyone in the volunteer team. 'Thank you!'

'Thank you!' They say to me. They know that people come and go on this type of mission. I'm not sure when or if I will be back. I appreciate the experience, though. I have a lot of respect for the organisation which was founded by a famous French comedian, known as Coluche. The charity is called *Restos Du Coeur* (Restaurants of the heart). I appreciate the charity, and also the people and companies who donate the food, *even* the fruit people, dodgy as the bananas are! *Merci, merci!*

18. METRO FRUIT

12th arrondissement, Paris.

I'm here in the twelfth district for five weeks, and I'm enjoying walking around my new neighbourhood. It's got a nice vibe, but I've got to say there are a lot of supermarkets. Just when you think there is no room for another supermarket, another one opens, and when it does, it's always busy. There's a never-ending demand.

I like the Franprix supermarket around the corner because they have a cooked chicken section. For two euros ninety-nine, you get a quarter of a chicken plus some mini roast potatoes. It's an excellent grease fest.

On the way to Franprix, there is a tapas bar on a corner, opposite the veterinarian. The tapas bar has a huge old wine barrel with stools on the footpath. I love tapas. I love *jamon iberico* and *croquetas.*

Across the road, there is a Korean restaurant. I stare at the menu in the window each day, longing for friends, friends that I can ring up and say, "Let's have Korean barbecue." Paris is a big city but I don't have many friends here, yet. However, I have discovered a group on Facebook called Hungry Expats, and I did go to a Korean restaurant with them! That's how I know I like Korean food. I shared a barbecue meal of beef and octopus (I know it sounded weird to me) and it was excellent! I knew I'd love it. It's the special sweet and spicy sauce that makes it.

Up the road, there is a chicken place next to the Taco shop. Prior to France, my perception of a Taco was, and still is, a Mexican taco; like the yellow curved corn shell. I eat them with minced meat, sour cream, and tomato. Thanks to two teenage girls whom I gave private English classes to, I found out that Tacos are different in France. They are a hot wrap, that is filled with chicken, minced beef, even *cordon bleus* (that sounds posh, but it's not) in a cheesy sauce.

I have had a French Taco since those English classes. I had one when I went to Nice for a comedy gig that ended up being cancelled, and nobody thought to tell me that. The joys of the business. I walked into a little Taco place run by an 18-year-old. He served me whilst watching the football on the large television screen on the wall. I sat at one of the plastic tables, and watched the football too, whilst I ate my beef Taco. It was gooey and surprisingly tasty. After, I went for a long walk towards the seafront, passing ice cream shops along the way. I studied each ice cream flavour on offer.

I digress. The chicken shop in Paris the twelfth near the metro, looks bitty. It only has room for two plastic tables inside. When I went in the other day, there were only a few pieces of chicken on display in the hot metal dish. You would think shop owners would want to make sure the bay marine is at least enticing to shoppers. But these guys.. (French shoulder shrug). Anyway, I was hungry, so I ordered, without realising it, chicken fingers (I thought I'd ordered chicken pieces). I took them home and they were a delicious surprise, too. Fresh, hot, tasty. I'm a fast-food lover, what can I say?

Across the road from the Chicken Shop is the metro, and outside the metro exit every day is an Indian guy selling fruit. There are often guys outside metro exits selling fruit, even herbs sometimes. The fruit is cheap, so it's hit and miss with the quality. I don't think you can usually go wrong with bananas, but rockmelons are dicey. There's luck involved in this cheap fruit game.

I can't understand how the fruit-sellers make money, however. Their stands are so little. Just enough room for some bananas, strawberries, rockmelons, and mandarins. I don't know where their back stock is kept. Surely they would need to replenish? I wonder if there is another Indian guy driving around Paris to all the metro stations, stocking up his guys regularly with the fresh fruit. How does this work?

I'm impressed with the seller's dedication. They call out to people. If they see you even so much as glance at the fruit, they will say, 'Madame, only one euro. Cheap.' Cheap, yes. Love the fruit guys. Love them. We all need fruit, right? And they need quick getaways... ah, I've suddenly got it. I understand why their stands are so small. Because they get fined if they get caught because they are selling illegally. I guess they need to keep everything compact so they can pack up quickly and run off when they see inspectors coming. Fruit dudes on the run. Ah, bless. Everyone's hustling.

19. TUILERIES CHRISTMAS MARKET

1st arrondissment, Paris.

Donna, my Australian friend with a strong Australian accent and a strong Australian look to match, stepped out of Tuileries Metro Station. We met up and pointed to the twinkling lights and the small Ferris wheel across the street. 'Oooh, look there it is!' Rugged up in our winter coats, gloves, scarves, and beanies, we stepped across the street to explore the markets.

When Donna had suggested visiting the Christmas markets, I hadn't hesitated. 'Yes!' I love wooden chalet stalls, twinkling fairy lights, sparkly baubles, gingerbread men, large pretzels, sugar-coated peanuts, hot chocolate, and mulled wine. I love it all.

The smile is glued to my cold face as we stroll past the German stand with its giant hot sausages. I salivate immediately.

'Let's do a tour, first. Then we'll decide what to eat,' Donna says.

I nod. "Yes. A food decision cannot be made just because we like the first thing we see. Although, the sausages looked bloody fantastic. Look.' People dressed in heavy winter coats stand around huge old wooden wine barrels, used for tables. Holding hotdogs in their hands, they wipe mustard from their lips. Ah! I inhale the Christmas Market air.

In the dark of the night, lights sparkle and twinkle on the chalet stalls. Beautiful homemade crafts can be seen in every direction as we stroll through. We turn a corner, and step into the kids' ride area.

Then, Donna says, 'Look! Punch!'

We are magnetised. Our feet take us straight to the punch. My eyes rest on the passionfruit seeds floating in the huge bowl of orange liquid. I rarely drink these days, but I know in this moment that I will drink this punch. The Martinique stall (first time I've seen a Martinique stall at a Christmas market) is also selling hot food. They offer rice and goat's meat.

My eyes stay fixed on the passionfruit seeds. My nose sniffs. I can smell the rum mixed with the orange. I look to the lady. *'Bonsoir. Un punch, s'il vous plait.'*

The woman serves my drink with a true smile, and I feel the joy of the island as she hands me my punch.

Donna gets a punch too, and we do a quick tour around the children's ride section. It's really small. These Tuileries Garden Christmas markets on the whole are small, but it's got all the essentials, even a mini ice rink with wooden animals for children to hold onto as they skate. Two-year-olds and three-year-olds wrapped so tightly in thick coats, beanies, and scarves that only their fat cheeks are visible, hold on to the animals as they skate/walk on the ice. A whole lot of super cuteness is going on in the rink.

Mmmmm. The punch is good, but it's not as strong as I thought it would be.

We continue our loop around the markets, passing little wooden chalet stalls selling Spanish *Turrone*, handmade earrings, pictures and paintings on wood, and children's painted wooden toys. My eyes take it all in.

Soon, we end up back at the German sausage stall. Across the way, I see a caravan. A lady in the caravan is cooking onions on a flat hot plate. I wander over and read the menu on her blackboard. I run back to Donna. 'This is it. This is what I'm having,' I point towards the caravan.

Donna nods. 'Okay. I'm going to go back to Martinique to get the rice with meat. Let's meet back here.' She walks off.

The woman in the caravan looks at me as I approach. *'Madame?'*

'I'll have one sandwich, please.'

'With onions?'

I nod, and the woman gets busy preparing my sandwich. My eyes follow her movements. I lick my lips. This isn't any ordinary sandwich. I watch the lady cut off thick pieces of *foie gras* and place them on the hot grill next to the frying onions. Then, she reaches for the bread. It is similar to baguette bread, but softer on the outside. I know this *foie gras* sandwich is going to be amazing. I just know it. It is costing me twelve euros and I am happy to pay. My eyes stick to the woman and my *foie gras*. She turns my *foie gras* over. She moves my onions around on the grill.

I take my eyes off the grill for a second, to look around

for a place to sit. Wooden tables and benches are to my right.

'Madame?'

I look up. She is holding out my sandwich, wrapped in a napkin.

'Merci.' I take the sandwich. It is hot in my hands. Goooooooooooood. I walk to a table that has a couple sitting on one side. 'Excuse me? Is this half free?'

The couple wave me in. 'Yes, yes.'

I take a seat, and look down at the big sandwich in my hand. She's been generous with the *foie gras* and generous with the onions. Donna appears with her meat and rice in one hand, and a large plastic cup of beer from the German stall in the other. She takes a seat.

'Bon appétit!'

We tuck into our meals. I take one bite of my sandwich and my eyes roll in contentment. I wish I could eat at Christmas markets every day of the year. *Joyeux Noël* to me!

20. *BOUILLON CHARTIER*

9th arrondissement, Paris.

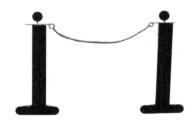

All the reviews say the same thing, "A Must Do. The food is excellent and cheap. It's one of the oldest restaurants in Paris. But beware, the service is fast and furious."

I'm a receptionist in a hotel just around the corner from the famous Chartier Restaurant in the 9th *arrondissement* of Paris. I have been dying to go because a lot of my clients come back, raving from their experience. International tourist heads nod up and down. "Yes, it's really very good."

I walk past Chartier every day to get to work, and every night when I leave work. The nights I finish work at 8 pm, I find there is always a queue out the restaurant entrance and down the street. People queue alongside the red ropes hanging between gold stands dotted along the footpath. Never have I seen this restaurant without a queue. Often, on my short walk from the hotel to the metro station, I have to step onto the road because there is no space; too many queueing people. That, and also loads of tourists wheeling big suitcases. This is a busy little street. Buses go up and down, and lots of cyclists, too. I always marvel at how the cyclists are not knocked down. It's crazy. Narrow streets with lots of buses, cars, Vespas, motorcycles, cyclists, tourists wheeling suitcases, queuing hungry people, and people like me, leaving work but having to burst their way through the Parisian obstacle course.

Today is our day to stand in the famous queue. Nikita and I had decided on a lunchtime Chartier visit. I had already warned her. 'There's always a queue. I can't promise if it's good, but it does have a reputation for being good. Apparently, it's real food, good portions, very French, and cheap. Three courses for fifteen euros.'

'Sounds good to me,' she'd said.

'But, I think it's in and out.'

'Sounds good to me.'

We met up ten minutes ago at the Grand Boulevard Metro station. We walked past the ice cream shop and the crêpe place, crossed the street, and we arrived at the little restaurant just next to Chartier. They must get the people who turn up, see the Chartier queue, and decide they don't want to wait that long. Nikita and I take our place at the back of the queue.

A waiter, dressed in black trousers, white shirt, and a red vest, walks to the end of the queue. He says to us, '*Bonjour. Table pour deux ?*'

'*Bonjour.* Two, yes.'

'This way, please.' He opens the red rope to make a gap for us to step out.

Oh, we are lucky! We follow the waiter, skipping past the larger groups of people in the queue before us.

The restaurant does not sit on the street. We must walk through a passage to get to it. Once inside, I look up. The ceiling is very high. My eyes scan the entire room. Everything looks very French, and kind of old-fashioned. The tables and chairs are brown, and of course, set very close to each other. There is no personal space going on here. Every inch of space is used up to cram more clients in.

Nikita and I take a seat in the middle of the busy restaurant.

'Mesdames, voilà!' A waiter drops two menus at our table.

'Merci!'

When he walks away, Nikita opens her menu, and says, 'Oh! Look, there it is, the fifteen euros for three courses.'

We order terrine on toast for starter, pig's cheek for main, and apple tart for dessert.

Each course arrives promptly, and as the reviews had said, it is good, filling, and the portions are decent sizes. The service is fast. The ambiance in the restaurant is one of go, go, go. Well-dressed waiters run back and forth whilst managing to look professional and organised at the same time. They all have a let's-get-this-done-but-at-the-same-time-enjoy-ourselves attitude.

I am impressed with the pig's cheek. I'm not sure what I was expecting. I didn't really think half a pig's face was going to appear on my plate, did I? Well, in any case, it's just meat, in a sauce. I like France and their sauces. Everything in a sauce. And everything with butter and or cream. Hence, everything is tasty.

I check the time. It's one o'clock, and the place is packed. This high-ceiling place echoes with the sound of glasses clinking, forks scraping plates, waiters taking orders, and clients chatting. It certainly has a good vibe.

This Chartier is a good experience because it is cheap, interesting, and quick. We pay our fifteen-euros bill, and meander through the close-together tables, careful not to bump into eating clients on our way out (I must be extra careful, my hips could take out a couple of seated unsuspecting diners if I'm not careful).

This was a good choice, although, I think the time spent organising our diaries, then meeting and queuing for it, took longer than actually having the meal itself!

21. THE COAT

Villennes-sur-Seine, Ile de France.

I'm standing in Monoprix supermarket in a suburb just north of Paris called Saint-Ouen.

My American friend, Ava, has been texting me all morning. "Are you still coming? What time will you get here?" "Can you pick up some pink and red crepe paper?" "The chef thinks we're not going to have enough tacos. Can you pick up some tacos from the Egyptian shop on the corner?" "Don't worry about the crepe paper, we're not going to have time. Just get the tacos." "We need beans. Can you get a couple of tins of cooked black beans. The Egyptian shop on the corner has them. And if not, Monoprix. What time will you get here?"

I feel Ava's stress. She told me four weeks ago about a *guinguette* on an island outside of Paris. (A *guinguette is* an informal bar/restaurant, often open air, where one can eat, drink, and dance. Usually in the suburbs)

Ava had said, 'Phillipe owns a little chalet on the island.

It's only a short train ride away from Paris. You must come! You'll love it. It's really pretty. You're only thirty minutes from Paris, and it's like another world!'

Ava had said that this island is made up of little chalets that people use as weekend homes, and in the middle of the island is a *guinguette*. She'd told me that she is friends with the *guinguette's* chef, Victor, and she'd suggested to him that she organise a Mexican Tacos Night for his restaurant.

Tonight is the night. Ava left Paris yesterday with Phillipe, her boyfriend. They have been at the *guinguette* all morning, preparing for tonight. Of course, now it's 3 pm and I'm standing in Monoprix looking for tinned black beans because the Egyptian shop had the tacos, but no beans. I find three tins. I text Ava. "I bring tacos and beans. See you in about an hour."

It's well-known that Parisians leave the city on the weekends to go to their country homes, and I've never really understood that, until today. After thirty minutes, I stand outside Villennes-sur-Seine Train Station, and my eyes ogle the difference in scenery. It's lush! I am surrounded by so much greenery.

Ava gave me directions to the island the day before: Turn right out of the train station, walk straight for 10 minutes. At the green sign covered in ivy, turn right. Walk under the little tunnel and turn left. Then, get to a car park. You'll see the river and a little boat station. Take the boat. She'd said, 'I'll be waiting on the other side.'

As I walk straight for 10 minutes, I feel an immediate change in my body. The houses on this hilly street are spacious and they have large, beautifully-manicured gardens. Everywhere I look I see beauty. Even the police station is pretty! A surge of well-being rises within my body. The sun shines and my soul sings. Thoughts of crowded, dirty Parisian streets float away.

When I reach the boat station, I say, *'Bonjour,'* to the other people already there. Then, I take out my phone and call Ava.

She answers saying, 'I'm here!'

I hear her. We all hear her. Not through the phone, but in real life. The people at the boat station and I look across the river. Sure enough, there she is, holding her phone to her ear, and waving.

The boat man arrives, and we all pile into his tin boat. I get in with my shopping trolley laden with beans and tacos, laughing, as I rock the boat. With each rock of the tinny boat, I fall more and more under the charm of this weekend getaway.

Ava greets me on the other side with a happy and huge smile. She leads me on a one-minute walk to the *guinguette*. I look around. It is indeed an outdoor bar, with a grassy area for dining overlooking the river. Directly next to the bar is a second grassy area covered by a large white tarpaulin. In this area, there are more tables and chairs, enough to seat 40 people. The outdoor, natural setting is a world away from sophisticated Paris.

Looking at the grass, the tarpaulin, the plastic tables and chairs, and the sun shining on the river, I say, 'I like it a lot.'

Ava smiles. 'I knew you would.'

She introduces me to her friends. 'This is Victor, and his wife, Nicole.'

I like them a lot, instantly. They are like their *guinguette*;

happy, relaxed, casual.

Ava shows me inside to the kitchen. 'Come Marie, come! Bring the beans and tacos.' Once inside, her stress returns as she realises how little time is left before the 40 guests arrive. Her voice gets loud. She shouts, to no-one in particular, 'Oh my God! I don't know why Victor said this was a good idea!'

I smile. I had prepared myself on the train here. I knew the next hours would be stressful. 'What can I do?' I ask.

Ava shoves a large baking dish of cooked pork over the steel bench to me. 'You pull pork. Throw any fatty bits into this dish, and you pull all this pork.' She looks at Nicole. 'Nicole, you do the apple crumble for dessert, and I'm doing the Ceviche. Oh my God, the fucking Cerviche! It needs to sit in the fridge for an hour before being served. Where are my knives? The sharp knives? Oh, fuck!'

I spend the rest of the afternoon pulling pork and chatting to Nicole, who does a million and one jobs for Ava.

Ava finalises her Ceviche but stresses more and more and more. She shouts, again to no-one in particular, 'Where is my fucking knife? Where did I put it?!'

We work, she stresses, we work, she stresses.

By 8 pm, it's complete chaos in the kitchen. Victor runs in from the outside bar area saying, 'Is the entrée ready? People are eating all the guacamole and chips on the bar! We need to get them seated at the tables and eating entrées. Quick, quick, quick!'

A pretty young woman called Marie, about 25 years old, has come to help. Marie, Nicole, and I get busy scooping Cerviche into little bowls.

Vincent counts the bowls, then looks at the Cerviche. His face drops. 'There isn't going to be enough!' He scoops Cerviche out of the little bowls and redistributes. Then he shouts, 'Go, go, go!' He waves for Marie, Nicole, and me to take the entrées out.

Outside, I note that Phillipe and Victor have cleaned all the plastic tables and hung up coloured lights under the white tarpaulin. They also lit a couple of tall, mushroom-like heaters, one in each corner, as it is November. The weekend Parisian people sit at the long plastic tables, chatting and drinking. They are in weekend mode.

Marie, Nicole, and I run back and forth delivering Ceviche. Then, we run back and forth recuperating empty Cerviche bowls. Then, we run back and forth with the main meals.

In the kitchen, Victor's face is red. He shouts, 'Hurry, hurry!'

Ava shouts, 'I don't know why you thought this was a good idea! Where are my fucking tacos? Oh, there they are!'

'Take out the sauces!' Vincent shoos us outside again.

I pick up a rectangular plate on which sits two bowls of green hot sauce and two bowls of red hot sauce. I run out to the grassy dining area and step towards a table. One of my red sauce bowl slides across my plate, and red sauce flies into the air. I watch in slow-motion horror as red splotches of hot sauce fly through the air and land all down the back of a pretty pastel pink coat. I'm talking a flicker of sauce, but big, fat, splotches of red sauce. My face remains frozen as I try to digest what is happening. The woman, to whom the coat belongs, doesn't move because she doesn't feel it, but her 18-year-old son sitting next to her sees my face. He looks down to where my eyes are pointed, then he looks back at me. Our eyes meet. I see his eyes widen. My stomach sinks. My head throbs.

The woman with the coat turns around. She's beautiful. She's tall, thin, has long blonde hair, and blue eyes. She is about 40 years old. I'm frozen as I stare at her beauty, then I jolt, then I release my verbal diarrhea. 'I am so sorry! I apologise! I will pay for all costs. I am so, so, so sorry.'

The beauty stands, and I watch her turn to look at her coat. I want to die. I don't want to be here. I say, 'I'll go and get something.'

I race into the chaos of the kitchen, and over the noise, say, 'Do we have tissues? Do we have wet wipes?' I look amidst the piles of plates and hot food spread across steel benches. I search left and right, right and left. Nobody answers. Everyone is too busy shouting over each other, stressing, and getting food in and out. Fuck. I turn around and around. Finally, I find paper towels. When I race back outside, the beautiful woman is standing at the bar. She has come around inside the bar to use the tap and sink.

I extend my hands with my tissues. She takes them, and wipes as the water falls onto her coat. She gently wipes off the sauce. We are both astonished as the red sauce washes right off her light pink coat. I continue my verbal diarrhea apologies, but she says, 'It's okay. See? It's washing off. I think it's going to be okay.'

I'm not convinced. 'I will pay for your costs. Please, if you see it has stained tomorrow, come back, I'll be here. I'll pay.'

Gentleness oozes from her. Her voice is soft. Her smile is warm. 'I think it's going to be okay. See? It's washing off.' She stands in her pretty blue floral dress, smiling at me, but I can't make eye contact.

The blood has fallen from my face. I can't get the look of her son's shocked eyes out of my head. I can't get the image of red splotches landing on her pretty pastel coat out either. I apologise again and slink away into the kitchen. I immediately dismiss myself from waitressing duty. I go and stand in the corner by the sink and the dishwasher. I demote myself to Dishwasher-upper.

Nicole, Victor, Ava, and Marie continue their frantic to-ing and fro-ing, getting forty dishes of tacos with side servings of black beans out. Next, they get busy serving the tiramisu with cream.

'The cream is no good on the Tiramisu!' Nicole runs in carrying a plate of Tiramisu in her hand. 'Stop! Stop! Use the other cream!'

Ava shouts, 'We need Margaritas! Someone give us Margaritas!'

In the corner, I load and unload the dishwasher. On my own, by myself. I have taken a vow of silence. I am trying to process my reaction. My body is hot with shame and I understand logically that everything is okay, but for some reason, I wish to burst out crying. I feel so disappointed in myself. I cannot believe it actually happened. As I scrape black beans off plates into the bin, I keep seeing fat red splotches landing on her beautiful coat. I move slowly and mechanically as I rinse dishes and load the dishwasher.

Ava comes to stand in the dishwashing corner. Smiling she loudly says, 'Marie, this is Franck! A good friend!' Ava points to Franck (he is in charge of making the margaritas). I barely look at him. I'm on the verge of tears. I cannot logically figure this out. I want to not be here. I want to not be experiencing these feelings. My body burns with hurt, disappointment, and shame.

I reload the dishwasher.

Ten minutes later, I hear Ava on the other side of the kitchen shout, 'What's going on? Marie is not a slave, you know! What's happening?!' She comes and pulls me aside. 'It's time to take a break. Sit with me. Let's eat.' She carries two plates to the little back room. I look at the tacos. All afternoon whilst pulling the pork, I had been salivating, dying to try the food, and now I have lost my appetite. I don't know if I'm going to make it through the dinner break without bursting into tears. I can't make eye contact with Ava, and I am still trying to process why I'm being so emotional.

Suddenly, Ava bursts into tears. She says, 'We've worked you like a slave. I'm sorry! I'm sorry! What's wrong?'

'Nothing.'

'Yes, we've worked you like a slave. Look, I got you a margarita.' She points to the yellow drink on the table.

'It's not that.'

'What is it?'

'Nothing.'

Ava bursts into tears again.

'Don't cry Ava. This isn't to do with you. I just need some time. Alone.'

She wipes her tears, but fresh tears spurt from her eyes again.

'Don't! I say to her, keeping my head down.'

'Okay.' She wipes her tears and stands. 'I better get back to the kitchen now.'

I spend the rest of the evening making sure my dishwashing corner is spick and span. Phillipe comes into my little corner and introduces me to his sister and brother-in-law. Again, I can't look at them. I berate myself, 'Why am I acting like this? What can't I let it go?'

'What's wrong?' Phillipe asks, once his sister and brother-in-law go back to the outside party area.

'Nothing. I just need to be alone.'

I feel that he is feeling for me and that he doesn't know what to do. There is nothing to do. I remain in my funk until the very end of the night when the plates have been washed and put away, the benches have been wiped down, a second bowl of Ceviche has been discovered in the fridge, and Ava has exclaimed, 'We didn't even serve the fucking apple crumble!' It is only now, in the now-empty kitchen, that I resign myself to the fact that I must join the others outside. I walk out and stay behind the bar. Guests are dancing on the makeshift dancefloor. Others are paying their bills to Victor behind the bar. I watch as these good, jolly people pay and leave.

'I'll take one of those drinks, please.' I say to Ava. I see she has been making special alcoholic concoctions for Nicole and herself in the back room.

Ava smiles, realising I'm slowly coming out of it. This is when I notice the angelic woman and her husband at the bar. They are paying their bill to Victor. I take a breath and walk around the bar to them. She smiles when she sees me. I see her reassurance. Her smile tells me that it really is alright, and it really isn't a problem. I offer my thanks to her for her gracious reaction to what was such a silly accident. She is so calm, so pretty, so angelic. I feel a weight lift off my shoulders as she and her husband leave.

When I get back to the bar, Ava hands me something very cold, very sweet, and very, very strong. Mmmmmmmmmm. I'm still going to need about three more of these.

22. CHINA TOWN

11th arrondissement, Belleville, Paris.

I'm addicted to duck, the orange ones that hang upside down from steel hooks in Chinese restaurants. What is it that makes them look so orange? I'm addicted to vermicelli rice noodles, too. So, it's off to Belleville for me. I take the Metro and get off at Republic. In the wide plaza, I pass couples Salsa dancing to music blasting from a cd player on the floor. I walk up the short street, past the kebab shops where men hang out the window and leer. Some of them not only leer, they say stuff, but my mind is locked in Ignore Mode before I even get to them. I cross the street where the canal starts. I walk past McDonalds. (I went in once. They have a separate coffee bar. The pastries looked plastic. How can we be in France and have this type of thing happen?)

I continue up the street, past the shops that sell cheap women's clothes, and past the shops that have baskets out the front brimming with all sorts: socks, hats, plastic buckets, purses, sieves, and phone accessories. I walk past Goncourt Metro. I am nearing Chinatown. Why didn't I just take the Metro straight to Belleville? I don't think like that. I'm a woman of routine. I always go to Republic, and I always walk up. I also always go to the same Chinese supermarket. There are quite a few Chinese and Korean supermarkets in the neighbourhood. All of them are good. All of them have their special touch. I like the one I'm going to because they have orange ducks hanging in the window. I like to stare at the ducks.

Just before I get there, I see a pastry shop. I don't think it is French-owned. The portion sizes of the pastries are too big. The other reason I don't think it is French (and I could be very wrong) is because of the type of pastries they have. They don't have the "beautiful ones". They don't have the petite strawberry tarts. They have oversized strawberry tarts, and they are not beautiful enough. Plus, there are no choux pastries: no *Religeuses*, no *Éclaires*, no *Chouquettes*. Instead, there are lots of sponge cakes with lots of cream. I like sponge cake. I like cream. I make a mental note to come back here. I continue. I cross the street.

The supermarket sits on the corner. Every time I go, no matter what time, it's busy. Today is no exception. People everywhere. As I walk in, I see young Asian women sitting at the cash registers. As customers walk in with their shopping trolleys, these young women shout, 'Leave trolley at the door! At the door! Leave trolley!' They don't look at the customers as they shout, because they are multi-tasking. They are ringing up the till at the same time. Behind the shouty cashiers is the cooked section. I see an older Asian man standing at the bay-marine section, just by the window with the hanging ducks. Very good. I relax. The plan is to make my way through the supermarket, and check out the duck on the way out.

I start with the vegetable section, and not for the first time, wish I was more of an adventurous cook. Maybe one day I will be. I want to be able to pick up a long, leafy, green vegetable and be confident about what to do with it.

I pass the freezer section. Lots of big fish. Enormous. Look at their eyes. I don't know how long these fish have been here for. I would like to buy one however, one day. I believe I need to take a week-long seafood culinary course in the south of France first.

I keep walking. I get to the frozen dumpling section. I nod to the dumplings with reverence. I keep walking. I get to the noodles section. My eyes shine and my heart feels light. Here they are, my vermicelli noodles! A large packet for the same price a small packet would cost in my local Monoprix or Franprix supermarkets.

The soy sauce is just next to the noodles. I grab a large bottle. Can't live without it.

As I continue to wander through the supermarket, I sneak glances at the other shoppers. I feel a kinship with these people. We like the same foods. We have the same tastes. I feel they must be good people. Of course, they could be utter pricks that just happen to have good taste in food. Speaking of taste, in my opinion, Chinese restaurants in France, depending on where you are, not in Paris but more provincial, well, some of them have "Frenchiefied" their dishes. They have lessened the Chinese taste to accommodate the French palate. Thankfully in Paris, as in most big cities in the world, you find authentic restaurants. I went to one in the 13th *arrondissement* with a group of friends and ordered pork and chive dumplings. This was an authentic *and* no-frills restaurant (11 euros for ten dumplings). Our meals came out at all different times. Mine was the very last, of course, but nevertheless, delicious and more importantly, authentic.

Back to this supermarket. I walk to the cooked section. The man is chopping up a duck with a machete. I stare at the delicious meat. Then, I look up at the price board. A cooked duck is 18 euros. Hmmmmm. This is a luxury. Not sure. I don't think I can afford it this week. Going to put the duck on the back burner and promise myself I'll get it the next visit.

Why do I do this to myself? I know how much the duck is. It's the same price as it was last time. Seriously, why do I do this? I dream about duck daily. Get the duck.

I don't get the duck. Instead, I give the stern cashier my money, take my noodles and soy sauce, and hop across the street to the pastry shop. I don't have enough money for the duck, but I sure do have enough for an oversized, creamy, not-beautiful-enough cake.

23. MARKS AND SPENCER

Paris.

Okay, so this one is cheating. I go to Marks and Spencer food stores when I'm feeling homesick for London, or when I want trifle.

You would think it would be easy to make trifle in France, but it's not. For starters, I can't find the gelatin to make jelly here in Paris. I've looked. In London, you pick up packets of gelatin for under a pound. The same must exist somewhere in Paris, and probably does at an exorbitant price in an "expats shop." It's nuts. Cream is an issue here too. It's not *impossible* to find whipping cream, but it's not exactly easy either. I have spent a lot of time on expatriate Facebook groups searching for discussions about whipping cream. These discussions exist, and people have been helpful in giving suggestions like, "This is almost like the real thing." I've taken screenshots on my phone so I can look for these nearly-the-same-thing products when I go to the supermarket, but of course, my local supermarkets don't stock them. I maintain hope. I will find this nearly-the-same cream at some stage. In the meantime, we have Marks and Spencer.

I have an emotional attachment to Marks And Spencer because before Paris, I lived in London, and I spent many happy years in London. My English diet was, of course, completely different to my French diet, but it suited me. I like English cuisine. I like sandwiches. I sausages. I like trifle. I like crisps. I like packaged stuff. Now, I'm changing a bit. The more I live in France, the better and fresher I eat. It's kind of inevitable, at least for me. Thankfully, there are a few Marks and Spencer shops dotted around the city. I have frequented the one in the 14th near Alesia Metro, the one in the 5th near Cluny Metro, the one by Passy Metro, and the ones on Grand Boulevard in the 9th *arrondissement* (there are two). The one next to the Grevin Museum is the one I go to the most often. I like being in a familiar place. I never buy anything different. I am a creature of habit. But, I like looking, especially at the cakes. I stroll along the dessert section eyeing the cheesecake, the carrot cake, the velvet chocolate cake, and possibly my favourite, the coffee cake. All of them have such good icing.

The last time I visited the Marks and Spencer in the Levallois Shopping Centre in the 17th *arrondissement*, I'd laughed because all the sandwiches had yellow discount tickets on them. Rows and rows of discounted Egg and mayonnaise, prawn and mayonnaise, and chicken tikka sandwiches. They just weren't selling in this area of Paris. The funny thing to me was that the sandwiches were in the refrigerated section under a sign that read *SNACKING*. After all, an egg and mayonnaise sandwich couldn't possibly be an actual meal, right?

I've often seen many things discounted actually. I think Marks and Spencer works well in areas where a lot of expats live, but not so well in the areas where it is French-dominated. Perhaps they just don't know what to do with scones, pancakes, and hot cross buns. I do. And, I love discounts.

Marks and Sparks' trifle is really good. It comes in individual little cups or in a big bowl. I never get the big bowl although I should. I should get the big bowl, then stuff my face all in one sitting and hopefully that would make me sick, and I would never crave Marks and Spencer trifle again.

The staff who work in these Marks and Spencers are French. I'm convinced they don't know the true beauty that is Marks and Spencer. I'm sure of it. They think they're working in a supermarket. Please. It's Marks and Spencer; home to yummy food. The good stuff. But wait... I see more and more French people in the store. It's catching on. Could a chicken tikka masala ready meal replace a meal on a terrace of a Brasserie? Never. But, the masala definitely has its place.

I have only positive things to say about Marks and Spencer, however the last time I went into the one near the Grevin Museum, the white chocolate biscuits sitting by the muffins looked really thin and sad. I guess it depends on which bakery services which M and S store. Sometimes the biscuits are going to be "like in London," and other times, not quite. But the other stuff like the cheese and onion crisps, the McVitie's Digestives' biscuits, and the Peppa Pigs are the same, obviously.

The sad thing is that in recent times, because of Brexit, Marks And Spencers have had hiccups in getting their stock over to France. Today I walk into the Marks and Spencers near Cluny Metro in the 5th, and there are empty rows after empty rows, with an orange sign saying, "Temporarily out of stock." No more Indian ready meals. The masala is no longer. More importantly, no more trifle.

Waaaaaaah! No more of a lot of stuff. I stare at the empty shelves with a heavy heart. I've heard that a lot of Marks And Spencers may close down due to the changes Brexit has brought. This is a shame. I understand that I live in France and I love French food, but I also love the fact that my London food fix is easily accessible to me. I shrug (the French shoulder shrug). *C'est la Brexit Vie.* At least it's not Australian food I'm craving. At least it's not a 28-hour plane journey to get what I want. It's a Eurostar, just over the channel, journey. There and back in one day if you really fancy it! And, I do. I fancy a caterpillar Christmas log. And trifle.

24. *LES HALLES DE LYON PAUL BOCUSE*

Lyon, Rhône-Alpes.

'Have you been to the food hall yet?'

'What food hall?'

'Near the Gare Part Dieu. It's famous.'

'For?'

'Gourmet food.'

'A gourmet food Food Hall?'

'You do realise that Lyon is famous for its gastronomy, right?'

I nod. Yes. Yes. Of course. 'By the Gare Part Dieu, you say?'

This gourmet food Food Hall is soon to become my place of soothing. I have found there is something calming about walking up and down the food hall aisles whilst gazing at the food. The products are so visually pleasing, and there are a lot of visually pleasing people, too. Who are these well-dressed people that can buy gourmet chocolates, just like that? Or oysters and lobsters? Or pâté that costs an arm and a leg? Who are these people? Every time I visit, beautiful people are sitting around the oyster bar, partaking in white wine and plates of oysters. And yet, here I am, still broke, still a window shopper. However, I stroll around with the attitude of "One day... "

Today is the day! I'm starting off small. I'm meeting friends for a glass of wine and a plate of tapas at the Spanish place. I bounce in, but when I arrive at the Spanish tapas place in the middle of the hall, my shoulders sink. I might have made a mistake. My eyes scan for a space but people occupy every high table, and also all the high stools along the bar. I look left and right. It's full. People are lazily sharing wine and plates of *jamon iberico*. Judging by their slumped shoulders and happy smiles, they are not going to be moving soon. Shit. I'm early, though. Maybe by the time one-thirty comes around, a table may be liberated? Fingers crossed. I decide to do a tour of the food hall to soothe my anxiety.

I walk past the oyster bar. There they are; the beautiful people casually sitting around the bar with glasses of white wine and platters of fresh oysters on ice. Wow wow wow. It looks so good, so refined, so civilised. I reach up and smooth down the stray strands of hair on my head as I walk past. I think, "Yes, this is how one should be living one's life. A Saturday afternoon with oysters and wine," except that, much as I would love to love fresh oysters, I don't. I do love *jamon iberico*, though!

I continue my stroll around. The pâté place looks crazy good. I love pâté. I look at the price, and for some reason, I accept it. I do a little shoulder shrug. I've tasted good pâté. It's almost priceless. And yes, I know how it is made.

Next, I go to the store that sells all the international stuff. Inside they have all the jams and crisps from the UK. They have noodles from Japan, and they even have vegemite from Australia. You can get a little jar for a big price. Nevertheless, I like this shop because they have a display of fresh food like greek leaves stuffed with rice, samosas, and falafels. Everything looks fresh and enticing. Huge meringues of different colours sit on the counter benchtop looking ever so pretty. I keep walking. Another champagne and oyster bar with people sitting at the bar. *Mama Mia!* The good life. I keep walking, towards the cheese shop. The young worker inside sees me coming and steps out of the shop to greet me. In one second, I see his eyes flit over my jeans and loose summer top.

He says, *'Bonjour, Madame.'*

I nod and smile. He said *"Bonjour, Madame,"* but from the way he said it and the twinkle in his eye, I feel he meant something else. Oh la la. Age difference. Not a problem in this country.

I walk up the aisle, turn the corner, and walk back down the next aisle to the Spanish Tapas Bar. It is situated in the middle of the Food Hall, and accessible from both aisles. I stand, looking at the tables. People are still chatting, but their plates are empty, and their wine glasses are nearly empty.

'Hello, Can I help you?' a waitress asks me.

'Hello, yes. I'm meeting two people, and we're hoping for a table.'

The waitress points to the wooden bar area, where high stools line the bar. 'If there is no table by the time they arrive, perhaps you can sit at the bar?'

I nod. I look down the aisle to see if I can see my friends. I can't see them, but I see the Cheese Guy. He has walked through his shop and come out on the other side. He is staring straight at me, smiling. Okay. Okay. Okay. I look back into the tapas bar. Oooooh! There is movement! Like a leopard pouncing on her prey, I lunge and secure a high, rectangular, wooden table. Hurrah!

'Hi ya!' Sean and Jane arrive two minutes later and plant their bottoms on high stools.

'Good timing!' I smile to greet them.

'What are we having?' Sean takes a seat.

'White wine!'

'Yes!'

'And a plate of the *jamon iberico*!'

'Yes!'

I rarely drink alcohol, but I will drink if I'm in the mood and if the ambiance is right. I'm finding more and more right ambiances lately. Soon I will have to stop saying, "I rarely drink." The ambiance is definitely right here. Large fat cured legs of ham hang from the dark wooden ceiling, sparkling large wine glasses shine from the bar area, and soft music pipes through overhead speakers.

Shortly, our white wine and tapas are served. I take a piece of the thinly sliced *jamon iberico*, and place it in my mouth. I close my eyes in joy. Cured Meat Heaven.

I spend a fun hour with Sean and Jane. I smile as I listen to their English accents. I like the way they say things like, 'Oh my gosh, the ham is ever so good,' and 'Ooooh, golly, this wine is lovely.'

The wine is indeed lovely, light, and fresh. I savour each moment of my gourmet food Food Hall experience gourmet food Food Hall or just gourmet Food Hall? These are the types of questions that float through my head). I sit up in my seat as I look around. Have I become a beautiful person? I'm not sure so, but I make a mental note: "You can afford to do this. Not every day, but you can do this regularly, you just need to schedule it in. This is good for the soul. This is actually healing. This is therapeutic. And maybe next time, try the Cheese place."

25. KFC HUNT

Pierre-Benite, Lyon, Rhône-Alpes.

Alice is my 40-year-old friend from the French island of La Reunion. She really wants to try Kentucky Fried Chicken whilst she is here in big mainland France. She's never had it.

I'm also in my 40s and have been living in this temporary accommodation on the outskirts of Lyon for a month. Alice and I have become friends with 70-year-old Clementine, who has also been living here for a month. Clementine and Alice's partners are seriously ill. They are in the hospital across the road. Clementine and Alice lodge here, in the hospital accommodation house directly across the road from the hospital. I am the live-in receptionist of this hospital house/hotel. The two women and I have become quite close in the last weeks. We share dinners together, and I listen to their heavy issues. Then, I bring laughter and lightness to balance things out.

The three of us have taken to walking around the hilly

surrounding area. The ladies share details of their lives with me. Alice tantalises me with stories about her island life in La Reunion. She describes her spacious home and garden. I picture all the green tropical plants. Josphine equally tantalises me with descriptions of her summers spent on the island of Corsica. I'm a sucker for the Mediterranean Sea and the lifestyle.

It's on one of our strolls that Alice says, and not for the first time, 'Let's get KFC! I have always wanted to try it.'

I say, 'Okay. I don't mind.'

'Me neither,' says Clementine.

Alice jumps up and down. 'Yay! KFC! I know there is one nearby. It's probably a thirty-minute walk. Is that okay?'

'Okay by me. Alice and I can go and get it, and bring it back to the hotel, if you prefer, Clementine?' I look at my older friend. She is an attractive woman, always well presented.

'No, I'll come for the walk,' says Clementine.

Alice claps her hands. She is finally going to taste Kentucky Fried Chicken.

I'm happy to have KFC but I am not as enthused as Alice. I have been into some KFC places in Paris and the chicken is hit and miss, depending on which one you go into. Unfortunately, in all of the KFCs in Paris that I've been in, I have never encountered good vibes. How can they destroy KFC for me? But, in Paris, they have. Seriously, the last time I walked into a KFC, I wanted to buy two pieces of chicken. They said they don't sell individual pieces anymore.

My eyebrows had raised. 'What about a bucket?'

'No. No bucket. We just sell Chicken Tinders.'

'You're a KFC and you don't sell chicken pieces?'

'That's right.'

'Okay.'

And that was my last KFC experience in Paris, and I had imagined was going to be my last KFC French experience, but it appears not.

Alice, Clementine, and I stroll through the residential streets of Pierre-Benite, which is about a half hour from the city of Lyon (ironically known for its gastronomy). I spend a lot of time in overcrowded cities like Paris, so when I'm back to places like Pierre-Benite, where you have greenery and space, it brings me pleasure. It stirs up envy in me when I see spacious, modern houses with well-tended, large gardens with dogs running around. I feel like can breathe here.

The three of us walk through the streets, past the lovely houses. We walk till we get to the main street, where we see a bakery.

'Oooh, we have to stop in here. I need to get a *pain aux raisons* for Marcel,' says Alice, referring to her husband.

According to Alice, this bakery is famous for its *pain aux raisons*. She heard it by word of mouth. It seems to me that every single bakery in France is famous for something or other. It's always, "Oh, this bakery has the best croissants," or "Yes, this bakery does amazing choux pastry," or "The baguettes in this bakery have won awards."

Bakeries rule La France.

With a *pain aux raisons* tucked into Alice's bag, we continue down the main street, past the supermarket, the petrol station, and we eventually reach a group of shops. These shops are in a u-shape form, with a car park in the middle. Smack bang on the other side of the car park, a big red sign says "KFC".

I look at Alice. Her eyes are shining and her back is straight. She walks into Kentucky Fried Chicken as if she's walking into the church on her baptism day. I observe her. I can see she is overwhelmed. Her eyes fly to the neon board above the counter, and she starts doing what I hate the most. Being indecisive.

'I don't know. Should I get the bucket with 20 pieces, or should I get the meal deals? Oh, look they have Original Chicken, and Spicy Chicken. Wow! Maybe I should get Spicy Chicken? But, what is the normal chicken that everyone gets? Is it the Original? I think it is the Original. Look! They have a meal plan where you get fries with it. Oh, I'm not sure. What about you?'

Clementine says, 'I'm going to get a meal deal for one.'

I say, 'I'm going to try the chicken burger for a change. The meal deal.'

Alice is thinking of Marcel, her husband. She must choose for the both of them. This is a big decision. She takes a deep breath and walks up to the counter. 'Hello, I'd like...'

'At the booths.' The young girl at the counter cuts in with her deadpan voice.

Alice blinks. 'Pardon?'

'You place your orders at the booths.' The girl points to five lit-up boards in the middle of the store.

I'm unimpressed. She could have taken Alice's order.

We go to the booths and start punching in our orders.

I hear panic rise up in my friend's voice.

'Mine's not working,' says Alice. A drop of sweat appears on her forehead. She taps harder on the board. 'Mine's not working!'

Clementine and I huddle next to Alice and try to help, but she's right, the booth is not accepting her order for a family bucket of original pieces.

Alice puts on her brave face and walks up to the counter. 'Excuse me, I must be doing something wrong, but I can't order the bucket of Original chicken.'

'We don't have Original Chicken today, only Spicy.'

'No Original Chicken?'

'No.'

Alice slinks back to our booths and starts tapping in her order. She puts on a brave face. 'It's Spicy Chicken, then! Easy decision!' She laughs off her disappointment.

Meanwhile, I'm having a mental conversation with myself. "And this is why I hate these places. This happens all the time. And I swear the portion sizes get smaller and smaller. And the chicken is more and more dry."

We punch in our credit card numbers, then collect our wonderful chicken. Alice hugs her bucket of spicy chicken. Smiling, we walk out, and we stroll the lovely half hour walk back to our residence.

When we get there, Alice gets busy organising the

reheating of the chicken. I set up the table in the backyard. It's a really nice afternoon. The serene, green, surrounded-by-tall-trees setting is the perfect place for Alice to have her first KFC experience.

Minutes later, under the shade of the large trees, Alice picks up her first piece of spicy, crunchy chicken, and as she takes her first bite, Clementine and I watch closely.

Alice's face doesn't move. 'Mmmmmm,' she says. 'It's... it's... okay. It's okay.'

I say, 'Marcel is going to appreciate that *pain aux raisons*!'

26. THE GOOD BREAKFAST

Vaujany, the Alps, Isère.

My summer job is in a mountain resort not too far from the city of Grenoble. Vaujany is a village set in a beautiful, flourishing mountain and the scenery is fairytale. It exudes health and good vibes.

A husband and wife run the summer hotel where I'll be working. No surprise, the wife is the boss. On day one, she takes an instant shine to my two male work colleagues. She assigns them their jobs, working inside the restaurant. She takes a lot less of a shine to me. She assigns me to the corner in the kitchen. I am to be the Dish Pig. This does not bother me. I quite enjoy having a manual job, where you can see at the end of your shift, the results of what you've done. You can measure your work. Plus, there is no pressure. No dealing with customers. I like that.

I share a room on the top floor of the hotel with the hotel's cook, Miriam. Miriam is Belgian and doesn't speak much English. My Flemish is zero, and my French is basic. Miriam and I don't see too much of each other however, as we are always at work, and when I'm not at work, I'm hiking up the mountain with my two waiter friends.

From the minute I stepped into this village, I have enjoyed it. I love the summer atmosphere and the landscape is so very picturesque. Pink flowers grow in fresh dirt flowerpots spread across the hotel's balconies. Across the street, lush alpine trees generate clean, pure air. I regularly walk up the mountain and watch the pretty stream flow down from the tall waterfall. Without even trying, I radiate health here.

You know how, when you're happy, you can eat whatever you want, and you don't seem to put on weight? This job and environment are doing that for me! The hotel feeds the staff good quality food. Breakfast is what surprises me the most because I'm not a breakfast person. I wonder if that dates back to my childhood in Australia. My brother and I had to get our own breakfast in the morning, as my mother had already left for work. Before breakfast, my brother and I would open our budgerigar's cage so Johnny could fly around the kitchen for a bit before school. One morning, as I was about to dig into my Coco Pops, Johnny flew down and sat on the side of my bowl. Then, he hopped onto my floating Coco Pops and walked ever so casually across to the other side of the bowl. I think it was after that budgerigar episode that I may have started the "Breakfast is overrated" thinking. I'm not a breakfast person.

Having said that, this Vaujany hotel breakfast is, in fact, my ideal breakfast. I have to be up and awake in any case because I have to wash up all the breakfast dishes. Plus, the hotel has a wooden terrace overlooking the amazing mountain. It is a delight to sit in the sun first thing in the morning, eat good food, drink good coffee, and enjoy the view. I sound like an 80-year-old woman.

I'm someone who can eat the same thing over and over, and that's exactly what I do each morning at breakfast, because we can serve ourselves from the guest buffet. This makes sense really, as we are such a small team of staff. In fact, I've come to realise this is the secret to good seasonal work. Take a job where the company is small, and you will have more chance of eating the same food as the clients.

The breakfast buffet here at the hotel is like most European buffets: croissants, *pain au chocolats*, yoghurts, jams, cereals, different cheese, sliced meats, and bread. In addition to the baguettes, the hotel offers heavy, dark, german bread. I always take two slices of this bread. Then, I take two slices of Mortadella (I love the big circles of fat). I also take a little tub of individually packaged Nutella. I grab my milky coffee and carry my tray out to the terrace to enjoy breakfast under the sun. From where I sit, I see my coworkers running back and forth to the kitchen to refill croissant and *pain au chocolat* baskets, and clear tables. I place my fatty Mortadella on my heavy dark bread, and bite. Just delicious. I always start with the Mortadella, then I eat the Nutella spread out on the second slice of bread. The sugar hit is sooooo good. I'm in love. I'm in love with carbohydrates, sugar, and fat. Each morning, I'm in love.

I look up and catch my South African coworker's eye. He nods to the croissant basket. I see he has just filled the basket with freshly baked croissants. I smile, nod, and get up to get a flaky, warm croissant to finish off my most magnificent breakfast that was identical to my most magnificent breakfast from yesterday, and the day before, and the day before that.

I smile. I'm working as a Dish Pig, and I don't think I've ever been happier or healthier.

27. THE CHEESE

Macot, the Alps, Savoie.

I hold up a picture of a plane. 'And this?'

My beginner English students, who are French and about the same age as me, stare at the picture. They search for the word. I wait. Their eyes are glued to the picture. I can almost hear their brains whirring as they search, search, search for the word.

Eventually, Chantal, a mid-forties woman with short, fine, blonde hair, bursts out, 'PLANE!'

I nod my approval.

Chantal's whole body sags with relief. Her face is red. She looks happy and exhausted at the same time, as if she has just pushed out a baby, not a word. The other students congratulate her.

Manon looks more closely at my picture. In French, she says, 'Yes, but is it a Boeing 747, or is it an Airbus?'

I smile a wry smile. It has been my experience in France that I cannot say general statements to my French friends, like, "Oh, look at that beautiful tree!" because this is not specific enough for them. They will say, "'Is it a pine tree, or a eucalyptus?" I've had the same experience with nuts. In my English class. I asked them, 'Do you like nuts?'

They said, 'Which nuts?'

'Nuts.'

'Which nuts?' they repeated.

I saw by the looks on their faces that they were dead serious. I said, 'All nuts.'

They did the French shoulder shrug, then pursed their lips. Manon said, 'I like pistachios.'

Flora said, 'I like cashews.'

Patricia said, 'I like walnuts.'

So, I have learnt that, in my circle of friends in France, a plane is not just a plane, and nuts are not just nuts.

Fast forward a couple of months: my English course is finished, but I have remained in contact with some of my students. They have become friends, and I have invited them to my little apartment (next to the Deer Hunter) for dinner. I run to my landlord's chalet in the next street, and knock on the door. 'Hello, Madame Robert. I'm having a dinner party and am going to cook *Coq au vin*. Would you have a big casserole I could borrow?'

Loaded up with the correct cooking utensils on the day of the dinner party, I get ready. I'm not a confident cook, so everything needs to be at least organised. I nod, looking at my kitchen. It's all there. I am serving *Coq au vin*, then a salad, then the cheese, then chocolate mousse. It's the cheese that I'm excited about because I have eaten enough times at my other French friend's houses to know that you never just offer one cheese (and you certainly don't cut it up before serving). You need to have a thick wooden cutting board, and on that board you put three or four (or more) different cheese, in their entirety, and the person will serve themself. I went the other day to the supermarket further down the valley, in Moutiers. It has a large cheese section. (Moutiers is a hub town. Trains come into it, and buses depart from it going up to several well-known ski resorts. It makes sense that the supermarket has a variety of everything. They cater to the ski season chalet hosts coming down the mountain each week to buy food to prepare for their chalet guests.) Anyway, the cheese I selected are my favourites. I'm excited to offer my personal selection of cheese to my students-who-have-become-friends.

Knock! Knock!

'Bonsoir!'

They arrive at the same time. Flora, Manon and Chantal ("Plane!"). Flora brings the wine, Chantal brings the bread, and Manon brings the starter.

'Voila!' Manon pulls out a small glass jar of *foie gras*, and lays a small loaf of bread on the table.

'Ooooh!' We look from the *foie gras* to the small loaf of light brown bread.

Manon explains. 'With *foie gras*, you don't use normal bread. You need to have a bread that is a little bit sweet. I asked at the *boulangerie*, which is the good one.' She points to her loaf. 'This is it.' Then, she asks for a knife, takes the jar of *foie gras* and knifes the edges. The block of *foie gras* falls onto the plate (I, the uneducated savage that I am, would have left it in the jar and asked everyone to dig in). Manon slices a sliver of *foie gras*, places it on her little piece of sweet bread, and explains (to me), 'You don't spread it with the knife. You eat it like this.' She invites us all to take bread and help ourselves.

I watch the girls take a sliver, put it on their bread, then into their mouths.

*Mmmmmm.*Chantal nods.

Mmmmmm. 'C'est bon.' Flora nods.

I pick up my sliver, place it on my bread and put it in my mouth. I want to shout, "HOLY SHIT! IT'S DELICIOUS!" I want to add, "It's the most delicious thing that I've ever had in my whole life! Stop eating it! I want it all!" Instead, I say, 'Oh my God, it's good!'

Manon smiles, content that we appreciate her choice in *foie gras* and the all-important bread.

After the starter, it's time for the main. I serve the *Coq au vin* and thankfully, it is a success. The salad, next. This is less of a success. I put too many ingredients in it. I added tomato, cucumber, and kidney beans. I think I should have stuck to the standard lettuce leaf salad. But they eat it, saying, 'Oh, you've put in kidney beans. How unusual.'

Next, it's cheese time. I am so happy that I have a thick wooden board. I place my four types of cheese in their entirety on the board. For decoration, I place some grapes in the middle. I proudly take the board to the table, and say, '*Voila! Le Fromage!*' I lay my wooden board down with a big smile.

Flora looks, and says, '*Oh non! Non, Marie.*'

My face drops.

'It's not *Le Fromage,*' says Flora.

I frown, confused.

Flora studies my cheese board. She says, 'It's *La Tomme, L'Abondance, Le Beaufort, et Le Roquefort.*' She points to each cheese as she speaks. The others nod, as if this is totally normal.

I laugh out loud. 'You're right! It's never a plane. It's a Boing 747 or an Airbus. It's never nuts. It's cashews or walnuts. And it's not cheese! Ha ha ha! It's Beaufort, Abondance, Tomme, and Roquefort! Dig in, please!'

The cheese is appreciated by all. In fact, the whole dinner is a success. Everyone enjoys it and we eat well. I can't help but be left a changed woman, however, because of the *foie gras.* It was something magic. I may hunger for it for the rest of my life. (And, yes, I know where *foie gras* comes from and how it is made. Shit! Tricky, tricky, tricky.)

28. OJ CHAMPAGNE

Macot, the Alps, Savoie.

We stand back and hold our hands up to protect our faces. Samuel has just said, 'I'll open the champagne!' It's going to be a big popper.

I squint, shielding the 5 o'clock sun from my eyes.

Rose's terrace is a sun trap. She lives in the village 20-minutes drive down the mountain from where I live. The drop in temperature from my place to hers is amazing. I wear a jumper in my place, even in summer. However, the jumper came off before I even got to Rose's village, which nestles just above the valley. Everything is green in the village. Flowers bloom, trees grow strong and tall, and birds chirp. Mountains with dense, vibrant forests surround us on both sides. Much, closer, enormous, healthy orange pumpkins hang off dark green vines which are crawling up the fence wiring of Rose's neighbour's fence.

Pop!

'Wheeeeeeeeey!'

Samuel manages to not spill any champagne.

'Marie?' Samuel calls, waiting for me to hold out my glass. He fills it halfway. He does the same for Rose's glass, and his.

Arthur and Ines, Samuel and Rose's teenagers, drink orange juice. I hold my glass to 16-year-old Arthur. 'Arthur, can you please top up my glass with orange juice?'

The French family stares at me.

Samuel's shoulders square up. 'Orange juice?!'

Rose's jaw drops. 'Really?!!'

I frown. 'Don't you do that? Half champers, half orange juice?'

An emphatic shake of the head comes from Samuel. More than empathetic. He looks indignant. 'No!' He shakes his head again. 'Is that what you do in Australia?'

'Yes.'

'Oh.'

'Have you tried it?' I ask him.

'Never! We would never mix orange juice with champagne. You are raping the champagne when you do that.'

His choice of language shocks and amuses me at the same time.

Arthur stands, holding the juice. 'Do I pour or not?'

'Yes,' I nod.

The kid pours, and I offer my glass to Rose. 'Try it.'

She takes a sip and nods politely. 'It's not bad.'

I then offer my glass to Samuel. 'Try it.'

He takes a sip. He shrugs.

Okay, so it is not for Samuel, but I enjoy my half champers half orange juice on this fine summer day in the mountain valley. The air is dry, and the trees are overflowing with flowers and super fresh green leaves. Everywhere I look there is savage greenery. These mountains are not the manicured mountains of Haute Savoie. This is Savoie. These mountains are the wild type of mountains, in my humble opinion. A lot of the chalet owners in this village have large gardens full of all the vegetables and herbs you can imagine. Plus, they have trees: cherry and apple. Rose's next-door neighbour has a big apple tree growing up and over her front fence next to the super pumpkins. Rose's neighbour is also Rose's mother, so Rose is gifted fresh vegetables regularly. A lot of organic mama-daughter nourishing.

I stand in the sunshine, enjoying the vitamin D, champagne, and aperitif food. We've got the usual: cheese, olives, and *saucisson*. But there's something new. Rose brings a plate of radishes. My eyebrows go up. I haven't seen radishes at an aperitif before, but I think, "Why not? I would offer celery sticks and carrot sticks, so why not radishes?"

Samuel picks up a radish and a knife. He cuts two deep slits in the shape of a cross into the top of the radish. Then, he takes a huge knob of butter, places it on top of the radish. He pushes the butter into the slits. He offers the radish to his wife, who takes it, and eats it. My widened eyes watch her. Samuel takes the next radish, does the same, and holds the radish out to me. I don't know what to say. I don't want it. I don't want to swallow a huge knob of butter.

Samuel sees the look on my face. 'What's wrong?'

Rose notices too. 'What's wrong?'

I sputter. 'I-I-I would never think to put butter with a radish.'

'Really? It's delicious.' Samuel shares a smile with Rose, before looking back to me. He is still holding the radish out to me.

I look at all the butter on top. I say, 'Is it? Is it delicious, Samuel? Or are you raping the radish?'

A great big belly laugh bursts out from him, shooting straight up into the sunshine. 'It's not the same.'

'It is. You are taking something healthy, and putting a huge dollop of pure fat on it. Why don't you just eat butter?'

Rose starts giggling. The kids, in the background, ask their father for a radish with butter. They come over, holding out their teenage hands.

I know it's rude not to try something in France (I mean, Samuel had the decency to try my half champagne/half orange drink) but I simply cannot put a huge knob of butter in my mouth (not without bread and garlic at least). If the radishes had been cooked in butter, I would have zero problem. It's the fact that the butter isn't thinly spread out or in a small amount. It's a huge motherfucking chunk of yellow. I look down. I drink my violated orange champers drink. I shake my head, as strongly as Samuel had only minutes earlier. 'No. I can't do it.'

The radish has left me feeling surprised. It's not the first time I've been surprised with food at Rose's house, though. A year ago, I came to see Rose at 4.30 pm. We were deep in conversation as Arthur and Ines walked in after school, hungry, wanting their afternoon tea.

'Keep talking. I'm listening,' Rose had said, wanting to maintain our conversation, and taking on her motherly duties simultaneously.

I kept talking, and watched as she picked up a fresh baguette, cut it in half, then picked up a block of chocolate, broke off a huge chunk, shoved the chunk inside the baguette, and passed it to Ines. She did the exact same thing for Arthur. The kids took their chocolate chunk stuffed bread and walked over to the TV room. I'd stared. I had never seen anything so basic in my limited French life! My eyes followed the kids, and I remember Rose had said, 'What? What is it?'

I think I stammered. 'Isn't that a bit... basic? Is this the, "I have no time to prepare anything," afternoon snack?'

Rose had laughed. 'This isn't uncommon. Bread and chocolate is a popular thing to eat for afternoon tea.'

'What? With a chunk of chocolate shoved into dry bread, just like that?'

'Yes! It's good!' Rose had laughed at my astonished face.

I said to her, what she would to say to me when I introduced the idea of champagne mixed with orange juice. 'Really?!!'

29. ABONDANCE, CANDY FLOSS, KINDER EGGS

Plagne Village, La Plagne, Savoie.

A forty-year-old man sets up a long table with a white tablecloth in the little snowy courtyard, out the front of the ski school office.

I watch him. 'Ooooh, I like the look of this.'

I'm the receptionist for the ski school. Next door to our ski school is a ski shop. Then, next to them is a little supermarket, next to them is a TABAC shop, and lastly, there is a little restaurant. In the middle of us all is the courtyard where the man is setting up his display. I peer out the window again. What is he going to display? It's always food, but which food? I watch, I watch, I watch. I see him pull out yellow. I smile. It's cheese! Hoorah! He's cutting up cheese into little cubes and putting them onto plates.

I'm not the only one intrigued by the Cheese Man. Tourists wearing brightly-coloured ski jackets, pants, beanies, and thick gloves start milling around the display table. The man hasn't even finished his display!

Mmmmmmm. I realise I'm going to have to time this correctly. I can't run out of the office and leave it unmanned, at least not for long. I'm going to have to be quick. I'm going to have just enough time to get some cheese, and nip back. I look out the window and frown. The bloody tourists keep flocking to the display table. They pick up cubes of cheese, and put them in their mouths. They talk to the Cheese Man. I frown some more. The tourists are not moving away. They need to move away so I can make my move. I start praying. "Please let none of those cheese-tasters be ski school customers. I don't want anyone coming into the office in the next ten minutes. I need to get to the cheese. Please, let the phone not ring either. I need no distractions for ten minutes." I look out the window. The crowd is moving. Good. Oh, no. Kids have arrived at the table. They are grabbing the cheese. Oh, the Cheese Man is cutting up more cheese. Good.

The Cheese Man does not have the same manners as the Candy Floss Man. When the Candy Floss Man came to set up in the courtyard last week, I didn't have to go out. He had waltzed into my office holding an enormous pink candy floss bouquet in his outstretched hands.

'*Oh, merci!* The smile had popped onto my face as soon as I saw the sugar gift. What a nice, nice, nice man.

The Cheese Man, on the other hand, hasn't even as much looked towards my office. To be fair, he is surrounded by helmets, beanies, and gloves. The tourists keep reaching for the good cheese. I wait some more, praying that no one walks into the office and that the phone doesn't ring. As I wait, I pick up a mini Kinder chocolate egg from the bowl. The week before, the Kinder representative had come into the office holding a large sack.

'Oh! What have we got here?' I'd said when I saw the enormous sack.

She'd opened the bag to reveal lots of little bags of white and orange wrapped mini chocolate eggs. My mouth had dropped at the sight. 'Ooooooh, thank you!'

Since then, kids have been running in to grab handfuls of mini eggs from the bowls sitting on my reception bench. 'Take, take,' I say, because I have eaten too many eggs. Didn't even think it was possible. Even the ski instructors are rejecting the chocolate eggs. When they come back from their lessons, I hold out the bowl, and they push it back, saying, 'I can't. No more.'

I put a baby chocolate egg into my mouth as I look out the window, staring at the yellow cubes on the table. People are dwindling. I'm going to go! I do a quick scan to check no ski instructor bosses are outside. I dash out of my cosy office, into the chilly air outside, and skip over to the cheese stall.

'*Bonjour!*' I smile at the Cheese Man.

'*Bonjour,*' he smiles back.

'What do we have?' I look at his cut-up pieces of cheese.

He points down. 'We've got the local cheese, Abondance, here.' Then he points to the other side of the display table, 'And here we have the Beaufort.'

Oh my God, my two favourites. *Mmmmmmmm.* I pick up a couple of each. Oh go on, I pick up a third cube of each. I smile at the cheese man, and skip back to the office. I shudder as I go because it is nippy out. I run back into my heated office, my palms stuffed with my yellow prizes. I lay the cubes of cheese on my desk and make a little cheese mountain. *Mmmmmmm.* I stare at my goodies. This might be better than the chocolate eggs. I love love love Abondance cheese and I love love love Beaufort. There is a certain tang to both. Apparently, the taste has to do with the flowers and grass that the cows eat. On the other side of the valley, there is an area called Beaufort, and, no surprise, the Beaufort cheese comes from there. The Abondance comes from the next region over. I pick up the Abondance cube and put it in my mouth. *Mmmmmmmmm.* I nod and smile. Good. Very good. I pick up the Beaufort. I put it in my mouth. *Mmmmmmmmmm* Very good. Can't decide. I love them both.

I look out the window, to the Cheese Man. I wonder how much longer he will be there? Probably a half hour. I wonder if he'll notice if I come out at ten-minute intervals for my cheese fix? I'm suffering withdrawals and I haven't even finished the cheese mountain in front of me.

30. TIGER PRINT

La Plagne ski resort, the Alps, Savoie.

'Get on the back of my skis!'

'What?'

'Get on the back of my skis!' Laetitia, a ski instructor, is in fancy dress. She wears a 70s all-in-one pastel pink and blue ski suit that outlines her trim body. On her head, she wears a long black wig, and huge peace and love sunglasses.

It's 6 pm, and the ski resort is putting on a show for the tourists. Ski instructors have just skied down the wide slalom slope in fancy dress costumes, whilst holding coloured flame torches. As they arrive one by one, I smile at their costumes. We have the YMCA copper skier, the Cowboy skier, the Army Seargeant skier, the Fat Naked Body Suit skier, the bright yellow *Piou Piou* (chirp chirp) Bird Mascot skier, the Tandem Hippy skiers, the Clown skier, and the Old Savoyard skier in his knickerbockers and old wooden skis. For the snowboard instructors, we have a Beach Bum snowboarder, a Chimney Sweep boarder, and a Business Suit boarder, amongst others.

Tonight, the ski resort celebrates 50 years of the station being open. A lot has happened to this mountain in 50 short years. It has gone from being an area where people were so poor they had to sleep with their cows to keep warm at night, to being a full-blown ski industry attracting many international dollars. Many old farmhouses have become designer chalets.

Laetitia looks at me through her purple peace and love sunglasses. 'Get on!' She nods to the back of her skis.

I'm in fancy dress too, but not on skis. I'm a ski school receptionist. I'm wearing a black bob wig, oversized blue glasses, my mother's long 70s tiger-print coat, and knee-high brown boots. The mulled wine I'm holding has gone to my head already. Free mulled wine had been offered to the tourists as we'd milled together on the snow at the base of the slalom piste. Claude, my ski instructor colleague, and tonight, Master Of Ceromy, tells funny ski stories over the microphone, and happy, fun vibes spark like fireworks around us. Then, Claude invites us to make our way across the snow front, to the Mall, to the cinema.

'Get on,' Laetitia says for the third time, nodding to the back of her skis.

I place my right foot on her right ski and my left foot on her left ski. I hold on to her waist with one hand, and onto my precious mulled wine in the other. Laetitia pushes off, like a skater. Together, we skate across the ski front, passing my fellow receptionist colleagues, who are walking across the snow.

Inside the mall, everyone follows each other to the small cinema. We gather inside, joke and laugh, and watch a short film about the history of the resort. After the film, it is with high spirits that we parade through the long shopping mall. Cowboys, Sergeants, Policemen, Fat Naked Body, Savoyard, Hippies, Beach Bum, Chimney Sweep, and Super Heroes parade through the arcade, past the bakery, the souvenir shop, the pizza shop, and the sports shop. Shopkeepers come to the front of their shops to wave hello. It is a small community. Everyone knows everyone. We wave.

'Bonsoir Fabian!'

'Coucou Alexis!'

'Comment ça va, Ivan!'

'Bisous Patricia!'

'Salut François!'

We near the cheese and saucisson shop. The cowboys, army personnel, and hippies enter. It's too irresistible. The shop owner already has cheese and saucisson cut up into little pieces, ready to be offered. I take a piece of cheese. It is a local cheese, Beaufort. I'm by no means a food connoisseur, but I think this cheese must surely be world-class. How is it that a teeny piece of cheese can taste like heaven? My eyes flutter. Then, I see the saucisson. Ooooh. I pop a piece into my mouth. 'Oh my God! Good!' My eyes grow wide with joy. I look at Laetitia. We nod to each other.

'Good, huh?'

'Excellent!'

What is it about France and food quality? It's brilliant. It would seem that it wouldn't occur to them to offer anything less than excellent quality. When I have gone to my friends' houses for a Raclette (melted cheese over boiled potatoes, served with cured meats on the side), even though it is a simple, easy meal, the quality of the cheese and cured meat is always so good. Do they even have low-quality ham in the supermarkets? Yes. I've seen it. I do know that cheap sliced shoulder ham exists, because I've bought it. I think I'm the only one. I lived with my French friend for months when I first arrived in the area, and I have never seen, and doubt will ever see, cheap shoulder ham in her fridge. What I do see in her fridge is good quality meat, fresh eggs from her parents' chickens, vegetable and fruit conserves made by her parents, yoghurts that look like they've been individually poured into beautiful little glass pots, cream, and butter. Not the cheap butter. The good butter.

So, in our fancy dress costumes, I savour the good quality cheese and saucisson as I gaze around at the beautiful gift shop. It is charming, displaying red and white checked napkins and plates, homemade pâtè, homemade pasta, local jams, and local honey.

'Merci!' We wave and continue through the arcade towards the party hall. Ski instructors sing at the tops of their lungs, and wave hello to the happy spectators who are enjoying the parade along with the shopkeepers. I link arms with the bright yellow Mascot, Piou Piou bird (Cheep Cheep bird). It is not the bird that is attracting the people's attention as we pass, however. It is my mother's 70s Tiger Coat. Tourists have been complimenting me on the coat since we stepped into the arcade. The coat continues to get more smiles and people pointing at it as we parade through.

The spectators are not the only ones who like the coat. When we get into the party hall (aka the sports hall), I regroup with my ski instructor colleagues. It's the first time we get to properly look at each other's costumes, and their eyes go to my mother's coat. These guys have only ever seen me in jeans and long-sleeved tops. Now, they see me in a long, fake tiger-fur coat. It is tied at my waist with a large black belt. My instructor colleagues can't see what is underneath. They just get a peek of my black tights, then the knee-length boots. This seems to have intrigued a few of them. Their eyes travel up and down. My eyes, on the other hand, travel across to the long food tables to the side of the hall. Lots of saucisson, Parma ham, cheese, fresh salad (yes, green lettuce leaves), soft fresh baguettes, pâté, and ham and olive cake. Next to them is the dessert section where pretty chocolate and coffee eclairs line up in perfect neat rows next to perfect strawberry *tartelettes*.

My French colleagues do not even glance over to the food. I know their eyes won't look at the food until the speeches have been done, and the "Please help yourself to the buffet," is said. The Australian in me cannot help but look over. I take 60 seconds to mentally prepare myself for what I'm going to eat first. My brain goes to work. It occurs to me that if I could only plan my career, financial, and relationship goals like I plan my food goals...

31. FETE DE LA POMME

Macot, the Alps, Savoie.

Nine-year-old Lily, dressed in black and yellow stockings and a black jacket, flutters about in front of the chalet.

'Lily, you make a very cute bee!' I say.

To give herself more "bee," the kid sticks a large white paper flower to her bike handlebars.

Today, in this alpine village in Savoie, with Italy just a hop, skip, and a jump away, it is the *Fête de la Pomme* (Apple Festival). It's an annual event, and it's the first time for me.

'Do you want to have a go?' Sophie's father, Phillipe, asks.

'At what?' I say.

He says, ' At making apple juice.'

'Okay. Where?'

'Downstairs.'

'Downstairs?'

'In the garage. Come. I'll show you.'

I follow him past the vegetable garden and the tomato shed. We walk around the side of the chalet, to the garage. Phillipe opens two big wooden doors. Sunlight streams into the cave-like room to reveal a large, circular wooden machine looking very much like it belongs to the film set of Game Of Thrones.

Phillipe waves me over to the machine. 'This is the apple juice machine.'

I stare at the old wooden tub and the big wooden circle hovering over it. My eyebrows shoot up. 'It works?!'

'Of course, it works.'

I am worlds apart from Phillipe. He was born and raised in the mountains in France. He has lived his whole life on this mountain. Plus, he is a generation older. He grew up in an era where they did in fact make apple juice with this very machine because, go figure, that was the only way. In my little mind, when I think of making apple juice, I picture a production plant with sterilised bottles travelling along conveyor belts. I picture apple juice magically pouring into bottles and travelling further along the belt to get capped. But now, here, standing in front of this circle of wooden slats held together with two thick black belts of iron, I reassess. The huge tub sits on a tall square wooden table.

Phillipe takes a bucket of apples (from Sophie's apple tree in her garden) and pours them into the tub. Then, he starts pushing back and forth on the steel thing sitting on top of the tub. It somehow presses the apples together, and through a tube at the bottom, apple juice appears. A small stream falls into the container on the floor.

Holy Shit! Pure apple juice. This is how we do it, ladies and gentlemen (you know, cause it wouldn't even occur to me to use a juicer). 'Wow!' I say to Paul, with wide eyes.

He looks at me. He's not exactly expressive. He is a relaxed kind of guy: zen, cool, chill. He doesn't know how to take me. I don't think he's met anyone with such little knowledge of the land, food, and mountains. He takes a glass, scoops up the apple juice, and hands it to me. 'Taste. I'll give you a couple of bottles to take home later. Just don't drink it all at the same time or you will have to spend time in the bathroom.'

Once again, my eyebrows shoot up.

Outside, it is all happening. The main village road has been blocked off to traffic and two guitarists stroll down it whilst playing and singing. Kids in fancy dress skip behind the musicians, or ride their bicycles, like Lily Bee. Starwars, knights, fairy, and princess costumes follow the Pied Piper musicians. Further down, ponies carry small children around the wee pony-ride track. The kids laugh and wave at their parents. Grandparents take photos. Further along, 4, 5 and 6-year-olds sit very still at the all-important face painting stall. Meanwhile, the air is filled with barbecue aroma as food stallholders flip burgers and sausages.

In one of the food stalls, green apples overload large wooden wheelbarrows. A couple of Phillipe's apple machines are on display, and village men work together, pushing the steel bars back and forth. Apple juice pours out of their tubs.

Sophie pulls me by my arm. 'Come on! It's time for the parade!'

Crowds line up on both sides of the road and we race to sit on the stairs of the local school to get a good view. My head turns when I hear music from up the street. The first floats of the procession arrive. Tractors with big fat wheels come pulling floats decorated in huge red and blue paper flowers. Kids wave to us from the float. I laugh. A tractor was the last thing I was expecting. Don't know why. This is an agricultural village, despite laying at the bottom of a ski resort.

Next, it's the horses. *Click, clack, click, clack.* Hooves hit the bitumen. Four strong horses trot behind the tractor. Sitting in the horse-drawn cart, two women dressed in traditional Savoyard clothing; headdress, white shirt covered by a long shawl, and long black skirts wave to the crowd. A group of young children, also dressed in the traditional Savoyard costume (the boys in knickerbockers and long white socks), sit with them, waving. The next float holds a large, old-fashioned bobsleigh. Men and children sit on either side of the old bobsleigh. They wave to the cheering crowd.

Across the road, behind the floats, I see the mini farm area. Children pat baby goats, sheep, and geese with ribbons around their necks. It's the red ribbons around the white fluffy necks of the geese that cements it for me. I am one hundred percent charmed by this apple celebration with all its visual delights. In fact, all my senses are on overload, and the smile on my face is wide. But suddenly my tummy rumbles and I frown as I place my hand on my abdomen. Uh-oh. It's not possible, is it? Is Phillipe's prediction about to come true? I only had a little sip!

32. DANDY

Aigueblanche, the Alps, Savoie.

My friend, Nicole, lives high up in the Grand Aigueblanche commune. I drive up the unfamiliar twists and turns of this mountain road to visit her. It's Autumn so there is no snow on the deserted road. I reach the first village and I am forced to stop. The first house in the village is an old, large, farm-style chalet. The chalet garage door is open and a big truck sits out front, blocking the traffic (which is only me). I blink. Am I seeing this correctly? Huge, caramel-coloured cows come out of the chalet garage. The garage! The chalet owner directs the cows and they walk up a wooden plank and into the truck. I can't quite believe my eyes. How many cows are in the garage? It must be a magic garage, because more and more cows keep coming out.

I turn on the radio and wait out the cows. When Michel Sardou has finished crooning and the chalet owner has finished loading the truck, I am finally able to continue my drive through the quiet village. I drive past the old, stone, catholic church, and the cemetery next to it with its generations of mountain families. I drive further up, around bends, till I finally reach Nicole's small alpine village. Nobody's around. I feel like I'm driving into a ghost town. I remember her instructions to park in the little plaza where I see the water fountain she talked about. Other cars are parked, too. Old farmhouses surround the plaza. Like proper old. They appear to have remained untouched for decades. I take my time gazing, lost in the old-world charm. Suddenly, something nudges my leg. I look down. A Border Collie is licking my jeans. His tail is wagging.

'Hello, you.' I pat my friend who has come out to greet me in his sleepy village. Then, I phone Nicole. 'Hi, I'm here.'

'I'll be there in a second.'

A second later, she appears.

'Wow, you weren't joking.' I laugh, and we give each other the kiss hello on either cheek.

She leads me past the farmhouse on the corner, and down a steep path to her grandparents' chalet. Her grandparents are long gone and nobody had lived in the chalet for years. Nicole recently moved from Paris. Can you imagine, going from living in the 7th *arrondissement* to living on the side of a mountain, in the middle of nowhere? She pushes open the short, thick, wooden front door. 'Mind your head.'

I'm short. Have never had to lower my head to step into a room before. Giggling, I step straight into yesteryear. The farmhouse is exactly as her grandparents would have had it. I try to take it all in. It's spacious. Huge. I can see the appeal. The potential is crazy, as it is in all the surrounding chalets. One by one, old farmhouses are being renovated into amazing 5-star, modern, spacious chalets with floor-to-ceiling windows that look out to exceptional alpine views.

Nicole points out the small window to the farmhouse across the path. 'That house belongs to a guy in Courchevel. He's married. He comes most weekends to work on the house.'

That is the other thing about the mountains; a surprising number of men (that I know) know how to renovate houses. It's what they learn to do in the summer when they are teenagers. It's their summer job. My first teenage job was working in my large local supermarket, in the delicatessen, selling hot chickens from a greasy rotisserie. I burnt myself with hot oil each weekend trying to get heavy rods off the rotisserie, despite wearing thick orange gloves. The store's policy was that no damaged chickens were able to be sold, so... ooops, there falls a chicken leg (as I tug too hard pulling hot chickens off rods). "Oh, this chicken is damaged. Guess me and my co-worker are just going to have to eat it."

Anyway, here in the mountains, a lot of guys' first jobs are renovating old farmhouses. They learn how to build foundations, do electricity stuff, plumbing stuff, tiling stuff, and all the stuff. Then, when they grow up and inherit their family's houses or buy themselves, they know how to do a lot of the work. It's an incredible advantage in my eyes.

Nicole mentions the neighbour again. 'He's a good-looking guy.'

The way she says it gets my attention, because a second ago she said that he was married. I don't know how much of the stereotype, "French people have affairs all the time," is true. I don't know. So I don't know how to react.

She continues. 'He's friendly toward me.'

I nod.

She continues. 'I'll see what happens.'

I nod again. I can't believe that Nicole would consider it. Wow, look at me, all judgmental! I'm not sure about anything anymore. I don't know. I don't know. I know nothing.

'Coffee?' Nicole offers.

I nod.

'There is no running hot water in the kitchen.' Nicole says.

My eyes fly to the tap. 'No hot water?'

'No. We need to boil it, or get it from the bathroom.'

Despite the basic kitchen, Nicole sure knows how to cook. Her meal later that evening is crazy tasty. We eat sausages with vegetables which sounds so simple, but she's done some razzle-dazzle stuff to make it taste insanely good. She tells me the vegetables and herbs were given to her by her neighbour (not the married guy).

After the main meal, we have fresh yoghurt. Nicole explains that the yoghurt has really good, health properties in it. I'd made the cardinal sin of bringing a dessert that I'd picked up at the supermarket on the way (Gasp! I really, really, really should have known better. Never take a bought cake (or bought anything) to one of my French friend's places. Nicole had pushed my plastic, shitty supermarket cake to one side, politely saying, "Thank you", when I'd handed it to her. I knew there and then that I would be leaving with it in two days' time. I'd kicked myself. Of course, my friends are not trying to be snobs. They just eat differently. I have other friends who wouldn't mind the supermarket cake. Sort of.)

I offer to wash the dishes after our amazing dinner. 'I'll get the hot water from the bathroom.'

Nicole hands me a container.

No hot water, and no heating in the house, either. The old villagers are not joking when they say, "In the old days, we used to sleep with the cows to keep warm". Good Lord. No heating in these French alps!

I have all my layers on because Nicole had warned me before coming. Luckily for me, on the big bed where I will be sleeping, she has layered on the blankets, plus an electric blanket. I'm going to need it. It's bloody freezing.

The next day, we have an amazing breakfast of bread, jam, fresh fruit, and yoghurt. Again, it sounds basic, but it is divine. It's weird. Nicole eats simply, but what she eats is high quality. The bread is amazing. The jam is homemade. The fruit has been picked with care, and the yoghurt is that fancy yoghurt from last night. It is rich and creamy.

Nothing is from a big supermarket, like where I shop.

After breakfast, and another trip to the bathroom with the container for hot water to wash up, Nicole says, 'Do you want to go looking for *pissenlit*?' (pronounced piss-on-lee. Poor Lee.)

'Piss on what?'

'*Pissenlit*. It's a flower. It's good for food.'

I'm up for it. We get in the car and drive down, past the village from yesterday, and soon Nicole parks her car on one of the bends. We get out and walk over to a grassy patch by the road. Nicole holds a little knife, and points to the ground. 'See that?' I see a weed. With great care, Nicole lifts the *pisenlit* green blades out of the ground. My eyebrows shoot up. It would appear to me that we are standing on normal grassy ground that boar and deer roam over at night, but in fact, this is fertile *pisenlit* ground. I'm flabbergasted. This is how my friend eats. Never in a million years would I think to go onto a piece of land and look at the ground, to get that little extra something to top off my salad. But, here we are. And, we are being watched over by the Virgin Mary close by. I saw her statue yesterday, just past Bend Number 20. She stands by the side of the road, with hands together in prayer, under a small white cement arch.

Eagle-eyed Nicole bends from time to time to gently pick up green blades from the ground. I look around me, half expecting to see a hidden camera somewhere. What is so normal and natural for Nicole is so foreign to me.

What a surprising weekend, starting with the never-ending line of cows coming out of a garage, to a side of the road search for *pisenlit*!

(P.S. I find out later that pisenlit is dandelion. Sounds better in English, right?)

33. GIFTS FOR SPAIN

La Plagne, the Alps, Savoie.

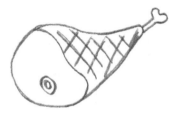

Years ago, I worked a ski season in a French resort called Meribel and my friends were a mix of Brits and French. I had a crush on a French friend. After work one day, whilst having drinks at a friend's apartment, my cute guy took out a saucisson from his bag. 'I bought this at the market,' he'd said, and then, looking at his mate, asked, 'Sylvain, do you have a cutting board?'

Sylvain passed him a board, and my guy took out his own swiss army knife. (Wow! Who carries their own swiss army knife. Ooooh! Swoon.) He sliced the saucisson so finely, with the precision of a surgeon. I was shocked at how finely he cut. I'm Australian, and I grew up with divorced parents. My father looked after my brother and me on the weekends. He fed us good cheese and salami, but nothing was finely sliced. It was chunka-chunka-chunka pieces of cheese and chunka-chunka-chunka pieces of salami. Even my friends in Australia now don't slice cured meat as finely as this young cutie in Meribel. As he sliced, he'd said, 'I chose this one because it has walnuts in it. See?'

Since that Meribel day, I've loved saucisson. And, also since that day, I've realised most people in France cut saucisson finely. (I have a flashback to an afterwork drinks event where I turned up with the cheapest saucisson from the supermarket; the no-brand kind. It was so cheap that when I cut it, it wouldn't cut finely because it was too greasy. We still ate it.)

What I'm trying to say in a rather roundabout way is that I have good friends in Spain, and I'd thought, "What can I take them as a gift when I visit? I know... saucisson!"

My heart and spirits lifted when I walked into the beautiful gift shop in Belle Plagne ski resort. Attractively-presented food spread across the space, including all the great cheese from the region. Lots of large circles, small circles, and triangular-shaped cheese. Lots of handmade chocolates and jams, too. And, lots of wooden buckets filled to the brim with saucisson.

I smiled at the man in the shop. 'I'm going to Spain. Do you do the vacuumed pack stuff?'

'Yes. Of course!'

I looked at the buckets. Too much to choose from: saucisson with blueberries, with walnuts, with Beaufort cheese, with Abondance cheese, with herbs, or just plain.

'I'll take one of each, please. Vacuum packed. And you better give me some Beaufort cheese, too.'

The man picked up the cheese, and indicated with his finger. 'This much?'

I'd nodded.

So, I have arrived in Spain, and am sitting in my room. My face falls when I cut open the vacuumed plastic because as I pick up the saucissons, they feel a bit wet. No good. Saucisson is supposed to be dry and firm. I wipe them off, then sort out which one is going to which friend. The blueberry one can be for Miguel, the walnut for Juan, the Beaufort for Eva, the herb for Pablo, and a plain one for Mari Pilli.

Miguel is an uncle figure for me. He will not be happy if I turn up to his house with food. I have to be careful how I word things. As I hand over the saucisson later that day, I say, 'It's only a small gift! It's just a token.'

He looks at the saucisson, and says, 'Why did you do that? We have saucisson here in Spain.'

On the trip home, I stop by one of my favourite cities, Seville. It is so pretty in the summer with the orange trees in the streets, wide promenades along the river, and the amazing *Parque De Maria Louisa*. Near the main bus station, where I transfer for the airport, is a large supermarket with an entire section just for jamon iberico. The smell of oak-fed pig wafts as you stroll past the counter, and huge pigs' legs hang from the ceiling. They have ham of all dates; the very very very cured, and the less cured. The display is clean and beautiful, and the ham isn't expensive. It's pork paradise.

Back in France, when I arrive at my friend's chalet for the *apéro,* I hand over a packet of vacuum-packed *jamon iberico* to my friend. (I should have opened the packet, taken out the slices, placed them on a plate, and made it look pretty. I never, never, never learn.) 'Here, I brought you this.'

'You shouldn't have,' says Stephanie, opening the ham.

I wait for the "We have saucisson here," but she doesn't

say it. She takes a thin slice of ham and pops it in her mouth. Her partner does the same. They look from the ham to me, with "the look". It was the look that I had wanted Miguel to give me when he tasted the blueberry saucisson, but he hadn't. Here, Stephanie and Lionel give me the "this is incredible!" look.

I take a thin slice from the plastic packet and put it in my mouth. My head nods immediately. *¡Y viva Espana!*

34. WEDDING SCALLOPS

Grenoble, Isère.

'Stephane, please, focus! What is the past tense of give?' I'd asked.

Stephane scrunched up his face in pain. 'Quoi? What? What? *Je ne sais pas*, Marie. Me not know!' Then, like a schizophrenic, he switched and smiled widely. He'd said the only phrase he knows in English. With a wave of his hand, he said, 'Get out of here!'

I couldn't help but laugh at his enthusiasm.

'Give, gave, given,' his wife, Isabelle, had said with good pronunciation.

It was obvious to me that Stephane is only taking English lessons with me because his wife really wants to. Knowing that, I have tried to make it as much fun as possible for Stephane but he just has no interest, no matter how interesting I try to make the lessons. He is more interested in teasing me. Stephane: the Clown. Stephane: the man who gets his English vocabulary from The Godfather movies.

Stephane and Isabelle have become personal friends. I was at Isabelle's 50th birthday party a year ago, when 51-year-old Stephane surprised all of us by getting down on one knee before Isabelle. Their 15-year-old daughter was the most surprised of all, I think.

Stephane invited me to their wedding over the phone.

'Marie, you have to come!' Stephane's voice beamed down the phone.

'I'll try. What date is it?' I look at my calendar. I am due to go to Paris for three months.

'August the 19th.'

This is in two weeks. Stephane is only giving me two weeks' notice.

Stephane's voice continues, 'And the 20th. And the 21st.'

'What?'

'It's a weekend affair.'

'Oh. Okay.'

'Don't worry. The hotel rooms are all organised.'

'What hotel rooms?'

'The hotel.'

'Which hotel? Aren't you having your wedding at the Town Hall?'

Every French person I know, which admittedly isn't a huge number, has their wedding at the town hall. Then, they have a party afterwards at a local hall or restaurant.

'No, it's in Grenoble!'

'Grenoble? The same place we had the engagement party?' (Grenoble is an hour and a half drive away from my mountain pad).

'It's a surprise where! Taxis will pick us up from the hotel and take us. We'll see you there!'

I thought back to Isabelle's 50th birthday party. It was held in an events venue on the outskirts of Grenoble. It was a closed-off area, and inside the large grey walls was a modern property decorated in grey and bright pink colours. It had had a bright blue pool, and a large terrace area with fake green grass for the barbecue and band. Isabelle, and all the guests, thought we were there to celebrate her 50th birthday, but Stephane had waltzed onto centre stage during her birthday speech, gotten down on one knee, and proposed. It was such a brilliant and emotional moment.

One year and two weeks later, I'm back at the very same venue. In the reception area, other guests keep coming up to me. 'Marie! How are you?' they ask.

These are the same people from the engagement party. How can they remember my name? I can't remember theirs! But I remember their faces and their stories. This happens a lot to me in France. I think it's easier for people to remember me because I have an accent. Everyone else is French. At least, that's what I'm telling myself.

Today, the taxis take us back to the grey and pink place with the garden terrace. The fake grass is still bright green, and the pool is still bright blue. The guests are in great spirits as we wait in the terraced area. The women and girls have dressed up in their best, brightest, and shiniest dresses, and the men look smart in suits. Stephane and Annick arrive onto the terrace, and everyone bursts into applause. We watch on as the exchange of vows takes place on the stage area, under the sun. Our hearts well up as we witness their declarations of love. Spirits are high, and the party kicks off immediately afterwards.

Stephane has gone all out with no expense spared for drinks, food, and entertainment. We gather near the bar at the other side of the terrace to enjoy drinks and nibbles. The skies are bright blue, the sun beams down, and snow-capped mountains in the distance overlook us. I look at the blue water in the venue pool and regret not bringing my swimsuit. Other guests brought theirs, and they are already in. I'm jealous. It's hot. At least, I'm lightly dressed.

Waiters, dressed in smart black trousers, crisp white shirts, and grey vests, busy themselves arranging things behind the long bar. Then, they flitter amongst guests. 'Champagne or Punch?' These waiters are extremely professional, but then again, I am not surprised. Waitering is a proper profession in France. There are schools for waitering. I think these guys have gone to them. Wow, they are smart. They might be the best-dressed people here.

Guests happily take glasses and start clinking.

'Chin!'

'Chin! Chin!'

Stephane's boisterous Best Men gather around their newlywed friend. They sing, hug, and monopolise their mate, rocking him from side to side as the barbecue is fired up at the bar. Mini herb sausages, chicken and onion skewers, beef and pepper skewers, and scallops are thrown on. Barbecued food aroma starts to fill the terrace and hungry guests look towards the barbecue area. Finally, it's time.

'Mesdames, Messieurs, venez!'

We gravitate to the bar bench to take our nibbles. As soon as I bite into one of the barbecued scallops, I am a changed person. Wow, wow, wow! Talk about perfect. Ooooh, I could not love them any more. They are marinated in a brown sauce, cooked just right, and heaven to the tongue. Oooooh, the combination of the texture and taste of the scallops, along with the champagne, and Stephane's loud singing voice, is too much. I praise the scallops as I put another one in my mouth. *Mmmmmmmmmmmmmmm.* How can scallops be this good? I find myself in a situation where greed may overpower my manners. I find I want to stand permanently by the barbecue and collect hot scallops as soon as they're ready. I want to block all the other guests from approaching. The scallops have the same effect on everyone because they, like me, are sticking close to that barbecue. Except for Stephane and his Best Men. They are on the other side of the terrace. Surrounded by his best mates, Stephane beams a smile across to me. He lifts his champagne glass high and shouts, 'Marie! Get out of here!'

35. *LAKE ANNECY*

Talloires, Haute Savoie.

I pull up in the car park. *Ping!* My phone beeps. It's a text from Christine. "We're here! We've planted ourselves right by the lake. You can't miss us."

I squint into the sun. With my bag over my shoulder, I slide my sunglasses up my nose, and breathe a happy sigh. I'm in beautiful Talloires, just down the road from beautiful Annecy. Christine and JuJu are already here. We'd made plans to meet for a picnic providing the weather was good, and there are blue skies without a single cloud.

I walk through the car park and over to the green grassy area in front of the lake. As soon as I see the expanse of blue water, I take a deep breath. Annecy Lake never fails to impress me. It's just too pretty. So blue. So clear. So big. Today, the sun is sparkling on the clear blue water.

The drive into Annecy from Albertville is dotted with charming French villages, like this one, Talloires (Talloires is perhaps the prettiest). Each time I drive along the lakeside road to get here, I see a sign for tennis courts but I never know where they are. They are hidden behind tall green hedges. This whole area is green, with camping spaces and bike paths. Magnificent houses rise up on the hilly terrain and overlook the lake. The entire area seems to shout, 'We're all rich and beautiful here! And we have beautiful houses, too! Welcome, and relax! It's too beautiful not to relax! And enjoy sports!'

I walk across the grass to reach my tall, brunette friend Christine, and her blue-eyed, sweet-natured daughter, JuJu. JuJu is six.

'Hi ya!' I smile.

'Hi!'

We give each other the cheek kisses hello.

'We got here before you,' says JuJu, swinging her long blonde hair around. She is dressed in a red swimsuit and there is not an inch of fat on her skinny-minny 6-year-old body.

'Have you been for a swim already?' I ask.

The little girl shakes her head. 'I've only put my feet in the water.'

I look over to the water. My soul expands with joy just looking at the inviting expanse of blue. I'm not the only one to appreciate its beauty. Everyone does. Everyone flocks here. Annecy and the surrounding villages are so busy in the summer, to the point where it is not pleasant to walk around some areas of the lake because there are too many people on bikes and rollerblades. There are too many people dog walking, ice cream licking, and not looking where they are going. Talloires is about a 10-minute drive from Annecy centre, so it's a little less crowded. Today, at this little park where red kayaks line up by the lake ready to be hired out, it's okay. It is busy with people picnicking, but not too busy.

I lay out my trusty picnic blanket. I hold up the fresh baguettes I've just bought from the super charming bakery in the super charming village just up the road. 'I've got the bread.'

Christine points to her Tupperware dishes. 'And I've got the ham, cheese...' she points to another little Tupperware dish, '...and some tomatoes.'

I look at the food she brought. Everything is in moderation. There is no surplus amount, it's just right. Christine is tall and svelte. As we help ourselves to our picnic lunch, I ask her, 'What do you eat every day?' (I'm always interested to see how other people eat, only because I have the feeling that I must be the piggiest person in the world. I certainly do not eat like a French person, as in three times a day and no snacking. I eat like an Australian person (or at least like many other Australians I know) in that I eat at whatever time, and I definitely continue eating after dinner time if I'm watching a film. Love the snacks.)

My friend shrugs. 'Just the usual stuff.' She takes a very small piece of baguette bread, and fills her plate with tomatoes, then one slice of ham, and one slice of cheese.

'But..., like, for breakfast... what do you eat?' I say.

'Bread and jam,' she says. She shakes her head as if to say, "Nothing special."

'With butter?'

Her mouth drops. 'Butter?'

'Yes.'

'No.'

'No butter?'

'No. Jam. Adding butter would be too much.'

I look over at the glistening water and laugh. 'I love bread and butter. With jam.'

She laughs. 'What do you eat?'

'For breakfast?'

'Yes.'

'Nothing.'

Her mouth drops again.

JuJu scrunches up her eyes as she tries not to get the sun in them as she looks at me. She wears glasses. I love little kids with glasses. 'You don't eat breakfast?' she says.

'No.'

'Ever?'

'No.'

'Oh! Wow!' The little girl takes a lazy bite of her ham baguette (no butter, of course).

I look over to the red kayaks bobbing in the water. 'I want to do that.'

'Me too,' says Christine. We should go together.'

I nod. 'Great idea. Maybe we could hire the kayaks, and then paddle over to all the little bars dotted around the lake and have a drink at each one?'

Christine laughs. 'Or maybe we could just enjoy some good kayaking, and at the very end, have *one* drink in *one* of the bars.'

Ahhhh, yes. *La vie française!* Everything in moderation.

36. CHALET HOST

Les 2 Alpes, the Alps, Isère.

£££££££££
£££££££££
£££££££££
£££££££££
£££££££££

Merci !

'Marie, you're going to Les 2 Alpes,' the Customer Service Manager tells me.

'What?' My mouth drops.

'You're going to help out a chalet. They're down a chalet host.'

'Okay. When?'

'Tomorrow.'

'Okay. For how long?'

'One week.'

'Okay.'

'You'll work with Jo and Steve. They're the main chalet

hosts, you'll be the helper. They are an older couple, very experienced and really nice.'

'Okay.'

'Pack your bags.'

'Okay.'

I admit I'm a little bit shocked, but not overly shocked. My job is to train new chalet hosts as the ski season progresses because the existing chalet hosts go skiing and snowboarding, fall, break legs and arms, and need to go home to England. Seeing as they do this repeatedly throughout the season because they don't learn, we need to recruit all season long for new chalet hosts to come from England. Hence, next week, we have a delay in a chalet host arriving.

When I say I have to train the new arriving chalet hosts, it is a quick introduction because they go into an existing team, so it's not too overwhelming for them. At the very start of the season, all the chalet hosts receive comprehensive training. We bring them together and put them up in a large hotel in one of the larger resorts and they learn to cook the menus we offer. The meal preparation process is step-by-step and each host should be able to provide very tasty, well-presented, and hearty (yet with budget in mind) meals. I've helped organise the training, but I've never given the cooking classes. Are you kidding? Me? Cook for paying people? My, my! I do know how to do all the other chalet stuff however, like bed-making and cleaning. In any case, this Les 2 Alpes experience is going to be interesting.

I am familiar with the Les 2 Alpes ski station. I have affection for it because it was the first ski station I ever worked in many moons ago. My Australian friend and I had arrived in the month of October, looking for work. We found jobs cleaning apartments. The boss man had looked at us and said, 'Are you sure you want this job? It's pretty taxing on the mentality.' We'd nodded yes and didn't understand what he meant until the next Friday, after a solid week of wiping windows and cleaning bathtubs whilst seeing nobody and talking to nobody in the ghost-town village. The repetitiveness of the work was excruciating. However, we survived, and both went on to get nanny jobs when the ski season started, but, both of us quit our nanny jobs in the first weeks into the season. We were not cut out to indulge young French children, nor their parents. So, I have bittersweet memories of Les 2 Alpes. I definitely remember spending a lot of time looking at the mountain, the snow, the valley, the cloud, and letting the beauty and magnificence of the true alps scenery envelop me. I was sucked in hook line and sinker by the scenery.

'Marie, hi! I'm Jo. This is Steve. Thanks for helping out.' The next day, a woman, young-fifties, smiles and introduces me to her husband.

'Happy to be here!' I mean it. It makes a nice change from working out of the office. 'So.... what will my duties be?'

"You'll be preparing three-course meals for the week, for a group of ten people. I do all the cooking. You'll help me in the kitchen with food prep. Just cutting up vegetables, making the desserts, things like that.'

I breathed a bloody long sigh of relief. How embarrassing would it be if the chalet host trainer turned up and presented a pretty shitty three-course meal of higgledly-piggledly cooked mish-mash crappy slushy crap-crap?

The week goes along smoothly.

I crash at Jo and Steve's apartment, which is just down the road from the chalet.

I love my job because I get to visit a lot of chalets and I am never unimpressed. Each chalet is different, and I am always taken in by each chalet's charming, warm, alpine atmosphere.

By the end of this week of cleaning three bathrooms, hoovering the salon, wiping windows, and helping food prep, I still like this Les 2 Alpes chalet. And, after observing Jo in the kitchen for the week, I think I would have been able to do the three-course meal. I have a lot of respect for the young chalet hosts who come over from England and do this. The first month is stressful because although their pre-season training is intensive and comprehensive, after that, you're on your own, and the first weeks of the ski season are Christmas weeks. The clients expect a very good standard, as they should, but of course, some hosts are still very much in the learning stage. It's one of those sink-or-swim jobs. It's also why it's one of those jobs where you bond very quickly with your fellow chalet hosts, ski reps, and resort managers. Everyone pitches in to help and work together where possible.

This week in Les 2 Alpes, our ten British clients are a dream. Lovely English accents fly around the chalet as they laugh and enjoy the food, the chalet, and their skiing stories. These clients are fun, polite, friendly, and cool.

On the last day, after the guests have left to return to the UK, I put the hoover back in the cupboard. Jo comes up to me and shoves 50 euros into my hand.

'What's this?' I look at the money.

'Your tip.'

'My tip?'

'They tipped us. We split the tips between us.'

Wow! Not only did I learn on the job, and got paid my normal salary, but I also got a tip! I now had enough to put toward the new ski jacket I want. Cool bananas. Thanks, skiers! Much appreciated!

37. MONSIEUR OBJECT OF ATTRACTION

Bourg Saint Maurice, the Alps, Savoie.

My friend, Chantal, lives in a valley surrounded by mountains and ski resorts. Saturday is the big turnaround day with clients leaving, and new clients arriving into resort. The roads are blocked the entire day because there is only one road going up the mountain, and one road going down. It's bumper to bumper as snakes of cars work their way down from all the surrounding resorts to join the one main road exiting and entering the valley.

'Marie, I've found you a job!' My friend, Chantal, had said. 'It's only a one-day job, but it pays 80€ cash in hand.'

My face had lit up. 'Thank you!'

'It's cleaning.'

My smile had dropped but, I'm poor. I'll do it.

'It's on Saturday, turn-around day.'

'I'll do it,' I'd said.

And I do. I go up, clean, and at the end of that day of cleaning, I say, 'Thank you for the lift.' I give a very weak smile to the woman who brought me down the mountain. Today has been difficult. Physically taxing. Crazy, really. We had to run around and clean like mad women. The French boss lady was a militant. She shouted orders all day. I'd watched on as the other women jumped and did what she said. The militant shouted, 'Clean faster!' and they cleaned faster. On top of this, they kept the windows open to air the rooms which is a good idea for the clients, but for the workers not so good. It is a ski resort, and snow does indeed fall from the sky, making the air quite nippy. So it's no surprise that when I enter Chantal's front door at 6 p.m. after my gruelling day, I enter with a blocked nose, sore throat, and I'm sneezing. 'Ah-choo!'

Chantal is waiting for me in the living room. She is dressed in jeans and a pretty top. She even wears light lipstick. I have never seen her with makeup. Ever.

'We're going out,' she says with a smile when I walk through the door. 'I'm inviting you to dinner.'

I stare at her. My nose is blocked, my head is thumping, my brain feels like it's going to expire. The last thing I feel like doing is going out to dinner. After working like an idiot for a shouting woman all day, I'm tired. I can't breathe properly. I certainly can't smell properly, and I'm pretty sure I've lost my sense of taste. I've definitely lost my appetite. I look up at my friend. Her eyes are expectant and shining. Her back is straight. She is wearing lipstick.

'We're going to a restaurant up the mountain. It's supposed to be very good,' she says.

I sigh because I suddenly realise why we are going to this

restaurant up the mountain. My friend, Chantal, is single, and she has developed a crush on the mountain restaurant owner. I've never seen her like this. I sigh. Surely, she can see how stuffy I am? My nose is red. I'm holding scrunched-up tissues in my hand.

'I can't smell,' I say, pointing to my red nose.

Chantal skips over to her little natural medicine cabinet and takes out a small bottle of oil. She drips two drops onto my wrist. 'Smell this.'

I take a sniff. 'What is it?'

'You can't smell that?'

I shake my head.

'Well, then you really can't smell. It's mint. It's very, very, very strong. Rub some on your temples. You'll feel better very soon.' She smiles at me.

I can see she thinks she's solved my problem and expects me to still go with her. Damn it. I'm staying at her house as a guest. I feel obliged. Shit. I look at her. She is smiling with her lovely lipstick. I breathe through my mouth, and say, 'I'll just go and have a shower.'

Forty minutes later, after the car ride up the mountain, and having spotted two deer looking for food in the snow by the forest edge, we step out of the chilly snowy air and into the warmth of the alpine restaurant.

'Wow, it's beautiful!' I look around at the sparkling lights and the wooden decor. Diners are seated at every table.

Monsieur Object Of Attraction and Recently Single comes over to greet Chantal at the door. 'Oh, hello. This is a surprise!' Monsieur smiles and kisses Chantal on both cheeks.

Chantal points to me. 'Let me introduce to you my friend, Marie. She's Australian.'

I nod at Monsieur and hold my hands up. 'Hello. I'm sick. Please excuse me not doing the kisses.'

I struggle to breathe whilst I check out Monsieur. He is tall and thin. He has curly hair. I like curly hair on guys. It's boyish.

'Please, let me seat you.' Monsieur leads us to the sole spare table.

Dinner turns into a concentration challenge as I struggle to keep up with Chantal's conversation. My body feels heavy, not just from the physical workout of changing 150 million beds, wiping down 150 million windows, scrubbing 150 million bathtubs, and vacuuming 150 million floors, all within the space of 8 hours, but because I order steak. I ordered it *à point* and I stressed *à point* (medium cooked) because once I went to the Hard Rock Café with English friends in Lyon, we'd ordered burgers cooked *à point*, and they brought us very well-done burgers because we are English, and they just assumed that we were English fools and didn't really mean *à point* and that we actually needed *bien cuit* (very well-done). Super annoying).

I really love steak and will eat it at any opportunity, but tonight I ordered it, knowing I wouldn't be able to taste it. Perhaps I'd hoped I would. But, I can't taste it, and I feel heavy inside as I know it is a wasted meal, and my friend is paying. Chantal doesn't even notice my lack of appetite. She is perky and luminous. Monsieur Object of her Attraction has been fluttering around, serving customers nearby.

He manages to come over to our table for a quick chat with Chantal. I look on, breathing through my mouth, watching my friend smile and laugh at all the right moments. I try to smile too, but it is too stuffy in the restaurant. There are a lot of people dining, and it is hot. My forehead is burning up. I can't taste my delicious-looking steak with has just the right amount of fat on it. I can't taste the chunky potato chips. All I want to do is step outside into the freezing air, but I am stuck. I look across the table. Chantal is looking up at Monsieur Object Of Her Attention, and batting her eyelids. Good for her. She really likes him. I begrudgingly nod and breathe through my mouth. I try to picture eucalyptus trees brushing my body, and I try to imagine the smell seeping into me and releasing my nasal complications. I try to breathe easily. I try. I try. Shit, it's not happening.

'How was the steak?' Monsieur Object Of Her Attention asks.

'Very good,' I nod, as he takes my plate away.

'Can I bring you the menu dessert?'

I shake my head. I'm a pretty greedy lady and am not one to turn down a glass of ice cream topped with nuts and sauce, but I think I've learnt my lesson here.

'Just the bill,' says Chantal. She flutters her eyelids.

In this moment, I truly comprehend that my friend is totally unaware of my situation, and in fact seems very pleased with herself. I think, in her eyes, the mission is completed. Good for her. I pray to cupid this has been a success. Fingers and toes crossed for love and clear nasal passages.

38. DAME BLANCHE

Vaujany, the Alps, Isère.

I am charmed by the beauty of this French mountain summer resort. There is a waterfall. I love waterfalls. My job in the hotel restaurant is to wash the dishes. The French hotel accountant, who has glasses, a moustache, and wears beige trousers, offered to take me to Grenoble on my day off, which is tomorrow. This is a generous offer because I don't have a car. I am "stuck" in the resort for the whole summer.

Jude, my sporty, fit, younger-than-me co-worker is not impressed with the accountant's kind offer. 'He sees this as a date,' he says. He picks up a tea towel and helps me dry dishes. He is the hotel waiter. He is supposed to be in the restaurant, serving guests.

'No, he doesn't. He's going into Grenoble. He knows I don't have a car, and that it's my day off, so he's offering a lift.'

'He thinks it's a date.'

'No, he doesn't.'

The next day, Jude stands at the front of the hotel: face stern, arms crossed over his chest, lips pursed.

'I'll see you later,' I say to him, as I walk to go down to the front of the hotel where Daniel, the accountant, is waiting in his car

'How long will you be?' Jude calls after me.

'I don't know,' I call back.

'Be careful!'

I turn around to face him. I yell up to him, 'About what?! It's not a date.' I wave goodbye, then run down to meet Daniel. 'Hi, Daniel! Thanks again!' I jump into his car.

Daniel and I take off. I wave goodbye to Jude who is watching us with eagle eyes.

In the car, Daniel says, 'Your boyfriend is jealous.'

I laugh. 'Oh, he is not my boyfriend.' I notice a little flash in Daniel's eyes, and I immediately regret having said it. Shit. Jude was right. He's in this for different reasons to me. And, now I'm stuck in the car for an hour and a half with him. I remain cool. Thankfully, after a few more questions from Daniel like, 'So, *who* is your boyfriend?' and my awkward answers with lots of *eerrrs, well,* and *ahhs,* I think he gets the hint that I'm not interested in him. I think he gets it.

But, thick-moustached Daniel has one last trick up his sleeve. Once in Grenoble, he offers to meet for lunch after his business meeting.

'No, I don't think it's a good idea because I don't know

where I'm going to be at 1 o'clock.'

Daniel nods. 'Okay, well, let's meet here at 3 o'clock. Then, we'll head back.'

I smile. 'Good idea.'

I spend a lovely few hours in Grenoble, strolling along the river. I take the cable car up to the château famous for the green Chartreuse alcohol that the priests make. Afterwards, I stroll through the city. I've just spent four weeks in the tiny Vaujany village with only the local Tabac shop that Jean-Louis runs with his lovely wife, and the bakery that I never visit because the bread and croissants at the hotel are so good. So, I am delighted to step into real, big-city clothes shops! Many, many, many clothes shops! Then, at three o'clock, I stand right where I should be.

Daniel walks up to me in his loose beige pants. He smiles. 'Did you see everything you wanted?'

'Yes! Thank you so much for bringing me. It's been an excellent day. And you? Get all your work done?'

'Yes.'

'Right, so let's go?'

Daniel points to a brasserie across the street, facing the river. A few customers sit, enjoying beers in the sun on the large terrace. 'Why don't we have an ice cream before we go?'

Shit. Ice cream. My weak spot. My shoulders sink. I already know what I want. Betrayed by my stomach, I accept, and order a *Dame Blanche*.

The Dame Blanche arrives in a triangular glass cup, and a

long spoon. Three scoops of vanilla ice cream sit inside, topped with fresh cream, and chocolate sauce. Daniel's ice cream arrives at the same time. Two plain scoops of vanilla.

I've been walking all day, and now we're sitting in this lovely, uncrowded terrace under the hot sun, overlooking the river, and I have a sugar beauty in front of me; the beautiful *Dame Blanche*. I savour each scoop, like a child.

I look around me at the other people on the terrace. Suddenly, I am filled with doubt. Suddenly, I feel like perhaps a French woman might not have ordered a big fat dessert in the middle of the afternoon? I don't know. I haven't spent enough time in France yet, but for some reason, I suddenly feel like I've ordered too much. Did I order too much? Shoulder shrug. Anyway, this is not a date, I don't need to impress him. Even if it was a date, and I fancied a *Dame Blanche*, I'm having a *Dame Blanche*. Life is too short. I dig into the cream drizzled with chocolate sauce. *Mmmmmmmm.*

Two hours later.

'So?' Jude stands by the door, in the same position as I left him this morning; arms crossed over his chest, lips pursed, face stern. He has just watched me get out of Daniel's car and walk up to the hotel front entrance.

As I pass by him at the door, I keep my head down and say, 'You were right.' I continue walking in.

His fists and face scrunch up. 'I told you! I told you!' He follows me inside.

I keep walking, and wave his comment away. 'Yeah, but I had a *Dame Blanche*. It's all good.'

39. GRENOUILLES

Le Monal, Sainte Foy, the Alps, Savoie.

I point to the paper on the low table. In my best teacher voice, I say, 'Stephane, for the fifth time... WENT. I *went*. Go, went, been.'

'I go to the office yesterday!' Stephane says with a beaming smile.

I shake my head, smiling. This man refuses to be taught English. He simply refuses. I know he is taking this as a joke. I know he is only taking English classes because his wife loves English, and also because he wants to hook me up with his cousin, who is very nice but about 15 years younger than me, not to mention very different to me. I know all this because we are having our English lesson in a bar/restaurant. It's a beautiful old building in an alpine village called Le Monal. Le Monal is on the way towards Val D'Isere and Tignes ski resorts. The thick stone walls of this restaurant give it its old French charm. Somehow the place is cosy even though it is spacious with large windows.

Stephane knows everyone in the bar, of course. Earlier, he had announced to all of them, 'Max and I will be in the back room, taking an English lesson with our English teacher!'

A man in overalls, and with a whopper moustache plastered on his face, had looked at me. I took a guess that this was Stephane's friend, the local carpenter.

The barmaid had held two thumbs up, with regards to our English lesson. 'Very good!' she'd said. 'Good luck.'

I need all the luck with Stephane. Stephane's cousin, Oscar, is tagging along for moral support and possible marriage. We sit in a room that looks like a cave, and I give a fun and relevant lesson. We practise phrases like, "Can I have another beer, please?", "Another round, please!", and "I've got the bill." But, Stephane is fixated on dinner, and before long he looks at his watch, and says (in French), 'Oh. English lesson is finished. Time for dinner.'

I gather my paper and follow Stephane and Oscar back into the restaurant section. We take a seat on high stools, around a high, thick, wooden table. All the furniture here is solid and modern.

The barmaid brings the menu. I peruse, thinking what to have.

Stephane smiles at Oscar and me. 'Frog legs?'

Oscar nods.

I play along and nod, too.

The barmaid takes the menu from my hands, disappears, and twenty minutes later, a wok full of raw frog legs appear on our sturdy wooden table! The barmaid places the wok on a fondue lighter thing. She lights the gas, and starts stirring the frog legs around in the wok. I do my very best not to let my jaw drop because:

a) I thought Stephane was joking, and was waiting for the menu to come back, and

b) These frog legs are raw. We must stir them until they are cooked.

I sit quietly on my high stool and resign myself to eat them. I will just eat them. I can smell and see garlic butter rising up from the wok each time Oscar moves the legs around. I tell myself it will be okay because they are smothered in garlic. The barmaid brings over a bowl of fat chips. They are proper, thick pieces of cut-up potato. They are the good chips. She arrives with a bowl of salad as well.

Stephane and Oscar are excellent company. Stephane is loud and cheery. His cheeriness is infectious. A *Bon Vivant* is a phrase often used in France to describe someone who enjoys life. Stephane is certainly a *Bon Vivant*. He likes to drink well, eat well, and play well. He runs his own successful business, takes his wife on gorgeous holidays, and spoils his kids.

'Stir the legs, Oscar.' Stephane points.

Oscar is closer to the wok than Stephane. Oscars stirs.

I have been glancing at these legs ever since they were placed on the table. They do indeed look like frog legs, and, as they cook more and more, the meat turns really white.

Stephane smiles. 'Let's go! Serve Marie, first.'

I lift up my plate, and Oscar places a scoop of frog legs on my plate. Then he serves Stephane, and himself.

'Bon appétit!'

'Bon appétit!'

'Bon appétit!'

I am sitting up nice and tall, but internally my shoulders are slumping, and I am thinking, "Man, I was so hungry too. I was so looking forward to this rustic mountain dinner." I smile, and lift up a white meaty leg to my mouth. I'm sure I must have had frog legs before. Surely, in all my years in France, I must have had frog legs, no? I know I tried snails once, but it's a distant memory. I watch Stephane and Oscar. I watch how they pick up the leg in their hand and eat it, like chicken. Then, they put the bones on the empty plate sitting between us. I bite into my leg. I am relieved. It's good. It's fine. I like the garlic butter. I can do this. It's going to be okay.

Stephane motions for Oscar to pick up the serving spoon. 'Oscar, stir them more. They're not entirely cooked through,' he says as he finishes the leg in his hand.

I freeze. Shit. Why did he say that? That's done it. The switch is off. I have trouble swallowing the bit that is in my mouth. I keep picturing raw frog in my mouth. Fuck. This is not good. We've only just begun. How am I going to do this? I help myself to some good homemade potato chips. I take some salad, even though you're supposed to eat the salad after the main.

Stephane's happy eyes are on me. He wants to please me. He wants me to love his favourite dish. I smile. I look down at my frog legs and pick up the one that looks the most cooked. I put it in my mouth and take a bite. It's no good. I keep imagining raw frog meat. Raw raw raw. I swallow slowly. I deliberately take my time, pushing frog legs around on my plate, whilst those two munch away, serving themselves again and again until the wok is empty.

Stephane wipes his mouth with his napkin. 'So, Marie! What did you think of the frog legs? Good, huh?' His blue eyes shine.

My eyes shine too, and my smile is wide and genuine. 'Excellent restaurant!' I say. It's true. I'm still hungry, but I am grateful for this experience.

40. THE FAIRYTALE CHATEAU LUNCH

Château De Feissons, the Alps, Savoie.

I don't know how many times I have driven this stretch of motorway, but each time I see the road sign, I smile. I don't giggle. I don't smirk. I just allow myself a smile. The sign reads, PUSSY. It's the name of the village. So what? The UK has Cockfosters. (Nobody wants to foster a cock. To my knowledge.) Today I am, again, driving along the motorway which goes in and out of the Tarentaise region. Striking mountains and forests line both sides of the motorway, and there is the Pussy sign.

A year earlier on the same road, a friend had pointed to a rocky patch, and said, 'You always see ibex here.'

Every single time I've driven along this motorway since, I've looked for them. I have yet to see one ibex. Maybe today. The rocky patch is coming up. I look to the right. I search for the goat-like animals with huge horns. Nada.

The clock in the car says 1 o'clock. Tingles spark pinging in my stomach. I smile. I have never been to this place before but I have seen it whilst driving. It's a château perched up high on the mountain in the middle of nature. I take the exit, and start driving up the unfamiliar windy road.

My ski season work colleague, Ana, had had the brilliant idea of having our end-of-season lunch at the château on the mountain in the middle of nowhere. How lucky am I, to experience this? I steer the car, winding around and around bends. I travel higher up the lush mountain. Finally, I pull into a large, open space with a gravelled parking area. My work colleagues' cars are already parked. Getting out of the car, I look up at the magnificent building before me. It's very much like a castle to me. In reality, it is a 13th-century fort that has been beautifully restored. It's an impressive, tall, old-stone building with thick stone steps leading to its entrance. It has turrets on both sides. The château sits on a large piece of land and looks down to the valley from which I've just driven up. Lush greenery surrounds me from every direction, and the sun shines from across the mountain range. I fix my sunglasses. It's late April, and today is very warm. I toss my cardigan back in the car.

'You're here! Come on! We're around the front.' My colleague waits for me to follow her around the side of the château where a large dining terrace, complete with white-material sun umbrellas, awaits. My friends and I are the only guests on the terrace. We are a group of twelve girls. I smile when I see them because they look pretty. They wear make-up, their hair is brushed nicely, and some of them are wearing skirts. I'm not used to seeing them like this. We've worked all season in a ski office wearing jeans, bulky jumpers, and hiking boots.

'Take a seat! We've ordered entrees to share. You just need to choose your main and dessert. We've ordered wine too. Red, White, and Rosé.'

I nod. We are all driving. This is going to be tempting.

Our waitress is a thin woman in her forties. She is dressed in jeans and wears hiking boots. She has no château airs about her. This is a mountain woman who happens to work in a château.

When the food arrives shortly after, it is, of course, presented beautifully. But it's not the food that is the star of the show. It's the château. Everyone has fallen under the spell of the château. It's like a dream. The sun is shining, and we are sitting on the terrace of a French 13th-century château dressed in skirts, wearing our hair down, and looking over to a massive mountain range across the way. I think this is possibly the most civilised thing I have ever done. I'm wearing Chanel No. 5, too.

The conversation around the table is happy and light. My colleagues and I are fortunate to work in hospitality and to receive this lovely perk.

'I need to pee,' says Nadia.

'Me too.' I stand to go with her.

We walk into the stone château, and it goes from bright and sunny outside, to dark and mysterious inside. We look up to the high ceiling in the large, old-stone room.

'Wow!'

The first impression of this front room is nuts. Our eyes scan the room. Silver knights' armour, complete with swords and badges, decorate the place.

'Oooooh!' Nadia says. 'It's like stepping back in time.'

The waitress/manager/receptionist/mountain lady smiles.

'The bathroom?' we ask.

She points to further inside, to the left.

We walk at a snail's pace, observing the decadent, red velvet old-world decor of the château. It does not disappoint. This is vision overload.

Back outside in the sunshine, on the terrace, the dessert arrives, and Michaela lifts her glass of Rosé for a toast. I can see the sun glistening through it. 'To the château!' she says.

We chink glasses. 'To the château!'

'Good choice.'

We look to our colleague, Ana. 'Yes, well done. You chose well.'

Ana nods, taking her compliment.

Michaela raises her glass again and announces, to nobody in particular, 'I want to get married here. This is where I will get married. Yes, this is the place for my wedding!'

Michaela is neither engaged, nor has a boyfriend, but we all understand.

'Hear, hear!' We chink glasses. 'To the château! To our French Life!'

THE END

My dear reader

I hope you enjoyed reading 40 Frenchie Flirts! It was an interesting project to write. Lots of fun memories.

If you liked it and fancy sharing your impression, I wonder if you might leave a quick review? Thanks very much for your time! Reviews help with gaining more traction/credibility/visibility as an author.

Best Wishes

Marie
Paris Connolly Writer website

In the series:

40 Frenchie Flirty Stories
40 Frenchie Foodie Stories
40 Frenchie Chez Moi Stories

Also, if you have/know people who have kids aged 8-12, you may want to check out this funny Middle Grade series set in the Alps. **French Marmot Dude Series.**

For kids aged 4-8 years, check out the **Colouring Books** in the same series (Magali Marmot's Snow Holiday, Magali Marmot's Raft Adventure, Bike Adventure, Paragliding Adventure etc).

Made in the USA
Las Vegas, NV
21 July 2023